# BURNING THROUGH THE WEST COAST

6,000 Miles,
576 Beers,
4 States,
3 Guys from
the East Coast
. . . and a Bag of Weed

# Paul DiSclafani

Illustrations by John Colquhoun

RED
PENGUIN
Books

*Burning Through the West Coast*

Copyright © 2020 by Paul DiSclafani

All rights reserved.

Published by Red Penguin Books

Bellerose Village, New York

Library of Congress Control Number: 202091822

ISBN

Print 978-1-63777-339-0

Digital 978-1-952859-54-0

Illustrations by John Colquhoun

*To Friendship and Family*

# Table of Contents

# Introduction

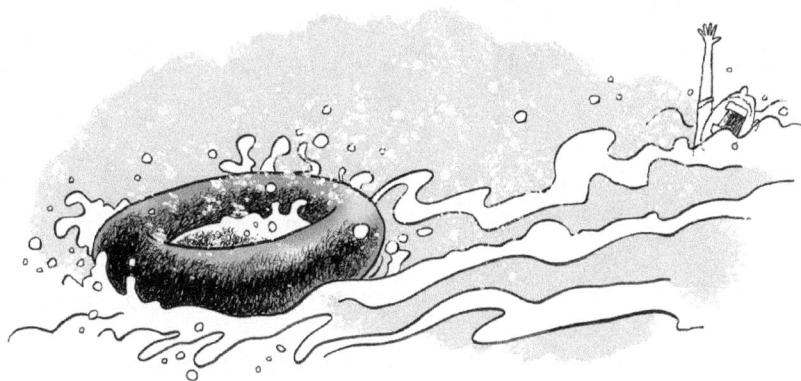

Cresting the surface like a desperate humpback whale, I snatched another quick breath before being drawn under again.

This was it, I was sure.

This was how it was going to end.

The rapids were racing around me, grabbing with unseen fingers and preventing me from thinking straight. With nothing to buoy me above the water, I went under again, realizing I had no control over the situation. The water was moving too fast for me to swim against it, and I couldn't reach the bottom.

The inflated truck-size innertube that obediently floated me into this mess was now racing solo in the same direction as I was, but just outside of my reach. Right behind it were two other empty tires, presumably having dumped their former occupants as well.

How did this vacation spiral so out of control? Two weeks ago, we were drinking beer and partying on Long Island, getting ready for a trip out to the West Coast. For my cousin Sal and me, this was going to be our maiden voyage on a plane, unlike Mr. B, who had flown a few times while attending Arizona State. The three of us had planned a West Coast adventure with stops in LA, San Diego, and Arizona. Now

*I was going belly up in an Arizona River, on the day before we were to head home.*

*"Let's go tubing," they said. "It's great, and you just float through the river. We'll get stoned, bring beers and sandwiches, it'll be cool..."*

*What could possibly go wrong?*

# Prologue—the Going Away Party

The Big Man had two gin-and-tonics poured and ready to go. The first one disappeared in two gulps, freeing up his left hand, which he promptly deposited in the garbage can full of ice and beer. It emerged, snatching a round bottle of "Schmidt's," like the claw from an arcade game. He was most likely going to be two-fisting all evening.

Someone must have loaded Springsteen's *Darkness on the Edge of Town* into the cassette player as the pounding opening drumbeats of "Badlands" began to scream from the speakers. That got Douglas, my brother Tony, and Mr. B, out into the middle of the yard, pumping their fists and shouting the lyrics slightly off-key. Soon, the Big Man joined them to form a drunken quartet.

It was a hot, sticky Sunday night in August of 1978. Although most Sunday evenings were reserved for tending our wounds from another out-of-control weekend, this party was in full swing. It was our last night before starting a California vacation. My cousin Sal (The Catman), Bruce (Mr. B) and I were flying to Los Angeles in the morning. Not that we ever needed an excuse for partying, but this was as good an excuse as any.

Sal and I had never been on a plane, and to be honest, I was a little nervous about it. Bruce had flown a few times while attending Arizona State University, so he was our local expert.

"Trust me, Disco," Mr. B assured me, using a nickname that stuck with me since fourth grade, "It's like riding a bus. I've done it a couple of times, and it was very cool. You just strap in, have a few drinks, and before you know it, you're there!" Then he smiled that mischievous grin that always seemed to get us into trouble. Somehow, I was still a little skeptical about being strapped into a flying metal tube.

With a last name like DiSclafani, I was given the nickname of "Disco" in the fourth grade by my friend Billy Cody, who wanted no part of pronouncing that monstrosity, and it has stuck ever since.

The party was kicking into high gear, and I was trying to score with one of the girls we invited. We spent many weekends following a cover band called "Thrills" and met several pretty girls along the way. But as usual, I couldn't make contact and continued to strike out. Instead, I grabbed one of the cheap "five-for-a-dollar" Phillie Blunt cigars that were sitting loose on the table and ambled over to the other side of the yard, where Peach and his girlfriend were rolling a joint.

"Can I borrow your torch?" I asked.

"Sure thing, my brother," Peach said as he handed me the lighter. "Pull up a chair and join us."

Peach was the lead guitarist in "Thrills," and this was a rare night off for the band. Long Island had become a hotbed for cover bands in the late '70s, and "Thrills" was one of the best. They were more than a cover band, sprinkling a few of their originals into each set. You could say they were a cover band with a twist. We became close friends with the guys in the group through our mutual love of music.

I jammed my arm into the ice-filled garbage can and swirled it around until I encountered something substantial. This was our version of "Beer Roulette." You never knew what beer you were going to come up with, but you were forced to drink your selection. I hit the jackpot with a Heineken and sat down to share a joint and some deep thoughts with Peach and Stephanie. Biting off the back end of the cigar and spitting it into the grass like a sailor in a black and white movie, I lit the other end of the stick before returning the lighter to Peach.

"Disco, you ever been on a plane?" Peach asked, while lighting up the poorly rolled joint and inhaling deeply.

"No," I stammered, "But, um, how bad can it be?"

"Oh man," he said, passing the joint my way, "Flying is great! It's the takeoffs and landings that'll kill ya!"

"Thanks, that was very comforting," I said cynically, handing it back to him for his turn.

"What are you guys doing for hooch out there?" he said, referring to the joint we were sharing.

"Nothing, man. We'll have plenty of weed when we get to Arizona and stay with those guys," I said, knowing what a complete burn we had planned. "Who knows, maybe we'll find someone in a park or something and cop a joint or two. They're supposed to be very laid back, friendly people, right?"

"Man, that's a drag," he said, taking another hit from the joint. "Might as well enjoy this tonight, right!"

Soon, a sweaty Mr. B joined our little group to partake in the pause that refreshes. "Where's the Catman?" he asked, while grabbing a fresh joint from the pocket of his Hawaiian shirt.

"I haven't seen him in a while," I said, pointing up at the

window to his room on the upper floor. The party was at his mother's split level, and his bedroom was way up at the top. "He's probably up there."

My cousin Sal earned the nickname "Catman" because he was so smooth with the ladies. He would appear and disappear while we were out partying, just like the Cheshire Cat from *Alice in Wonderland*, including that sly smile on his face.

Our conversation with Peach started to drift into different types of guitars and playing styles, as Mr. B and Peach began comparing notes. Mr. B was a musician in his own right, once playing bass in a band during his high school years. He still played a mean guitar on the side and had developed a special musician kinship with Peach. But once they started talking about chords and different types of guitars, that went right over my head.

I met Bruce in high school while in the A Capella Choir. How we ever became friends, I'll never know. We were total opposites. I was a loner and a nerdish kind of kid, while he was an outgoing, loud maniac. I guess opposites attract, right?

We maintained a genuinely symbiotic relationship over the years. Bruce was the yin to my yang, like Lennon and McCartney. He had a knack for bringing me right up to a line I never would have considered crossing on my own. Sometimes we stepped over it, sometimes I'd talk him out of it. Either way, it was always an adventure.

Although Bruce shared his name with our favorite performer, Bruce Springsteen, I always got the impression that he was somehow embarrassed by how his name sounded when people addressed him. In the late '70s, the name Bruce had a bit of a gay connotation to it. We called him "Mr. Bruce" at one point, later shortening it to "Mr. B." Although Springsteen succeeded in making the name Bruce cool again, Mr. B kind of stuck as his moniker.

After finishing the Heineken, I had to pee badly.

The downstairs bathroom just off the garage was occupied, so I stumbled up the stairs to use the one in the main house. Curiously, I noticed my friend Joe in the kitchen, staring into the open refrigerator freezer. He was rifling through the neatly wrapped items.

"Ah, here it is," he triumphantly exclaimed as I approached him to ask what he was doing.

He was dripping wet and naked except for a blue bath towel wrapped around his waist.

"Don't worry," he told me confidently, displaying his prize in one hand and holding the towel in place with the other, "As soon as I find a frying pan, I'm making steak!"

Sure, why not?

Not wanting to know the answer as to why he was wearing a bath towel, or the reason why he felt the need to take a shower at 12:37 am, I continued up the stairs to the other bathroom. It was just outside the steps leading up to the Catman's currently occupied bedroom. Sitting on the first step was a pretty blonde girl I didn't recognize.

Since the bathroom door was closed, I asked her if she was waiting to use it. "Oh no," she answered politely in a wispy voice, "I'm waiting for Sal," then pointed over her shoulder to the closed door behind her.

How nice.

Just then, the bathroom door swung open, and another pretty girl, this one a brunette with smeared mascara, stumbled out and sat down next to the blonde. I wondered if the Catman was giving out numbers like a supermarket deli, and they were waiting for him to call, "Next!"

By now, Douglas, my brother Tony, and Matty were setting up shots of Jack Daniels and topping them off with Peppermint Schnapps. It's a drink we concocted hanging out at a local bar in Massapequa, "Jocelyn's." We called it a "Snowshoe." The Schnapps added a layer of smoothness to the Jack, while increasing the potency.

"Here, here!" Douglas slurred through half-slit eyes while holding up his shot glass and spilling half of it on his shirt. "To the boys going to California!"

"And to all you assholes for not going with us!" answered Mr. B as we all laughed and drank.

Just then, Joe stuck his still wet head out the kitchen window and was brandishing a spatula. "Anyone want a piece of steak?"

We were legends in our own minds here on the East Coast. A hard-partying group of young New Yorkers in our early '20s ready to bring the party to the West Coast in the summer of 1978.

In reality, we were about to be three very hung-over young adults wishing we did not have a going-away party the night before we boarded a six-hour flight to Los Angeles…

# LOS ANGELES

# Los Angeles

LAX

Mr. B Working

Nice Hats!

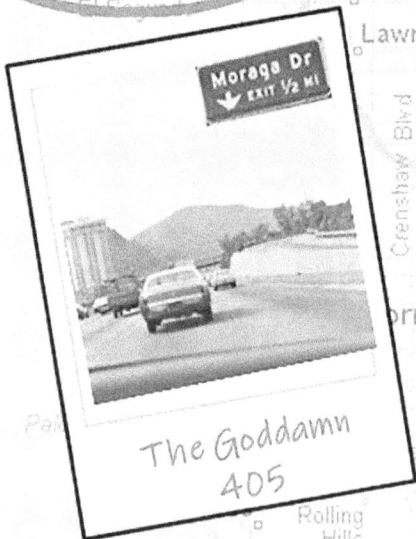

The Goddamn 405

The Catman

Disco and Jaws

The Poppa Do-Run-Runs

Old Time Cars

The Trip Planner

# the Flight to L.A.

Why did we drink so heavily last night?

I didn't sleep much when I got home from the party. Actually, I'm not quite sure when I crawled in my door. The last thing I remembered was it being about 2 am and enjoying the steak Joe had prepared way more than I should have. I can only imagine my Uncle Mario reaching into the freezer later in the week and asking Aunt Jean where the hell that steak was.

The alarm sprang to life way too early for my brain to process. Thank goodness I was already packed with just a few odds and ends to stuff into the bag. Our flight was leaving from JFK at 11 am, and my father insisted we get going by 9. Living on Long Island for most of my life, I knew all about the traffic on a Monday morning. With JFK about a 40-minute drive, he wasn't taking any chances.

"You better eat something," my mother warned as she was scrambling eggs for my father. I took one look at the sloppy, runny concoction on my father's plate and said, "No, thanks," popping two bagel slices into the toaster instead.

Like most Long Island families, we had fresh bagels every other Sunday. My mother always sliced the remaining fresh bagels lengthwise into three pieces, creating two ends and a middle. These were still available in the freezer for a quick breakfast. Apparently, I wasn't the only member of this household who preferred using any two "end" pieces. The remaining stash was littered with orphaned "middle" pieces. I painted a layer of cream cheese on them and slapped on my Mets hat to camouflage my incredibly wild morning hair.

Sal was sitting on the stoop with his suitcase when we pulled up. He looked like he had just rolled out of bed, which was an unusual look for The Catman. I made a mental note to ask him about the blonde chick I'd seen sitting on his stairs. Not surprisingly, Bruce looked even worse when we got to Pittsburgh Avenue. Bruce's younger brother Peter followed him out to the car, stopping to say hello while Bruce put his bag in the trunk. "You guys look like shit," he commented, seeing our faces and breaking out laughing.

"Just remember to pick us up, you Hammerhead," Mr. B reminded him, as he gave him a bro-hug. "Hammerhead" was (and still is) a favorite phrase from Mr. B.

The ride to the airport was quiet and subdued. Although I'd passed that airport hundreds of times, traveling between Massapequa and Ozone Park where my grandparents live, I was only inside once. As a kid, my father brought me along to see my grandfather off to Italy in the early '60s. Back then, it was called "Idlewild." Since then, it was renamed for President Kennedy and renovated.

As kids, my brother and I would always ride in the "ultra-back" of my father's Chevy station wagon. There was no greater thrill than driving past the airport on the Belt Parkway at the exact moment one of those giant planes was coming in for a landing at JFK. The final approach to the runway brought the screaming jetliners to within a couple hundred feet of us while stuck in Sunday afternoon traffic.

My mother always wondered how the plane, which weighs so much, could stay in the air. I'd laugh at her ignorance, knowing that science was on my side. But how the hell DID that plane stay in the air? Oh God, I hate her…

We pulled up to the TWA boarding area about 10 am and saw some guy outside of the terminal waving us over to him. He was announcing that we could use the new "curbside" check-in. Yeah, like we would fall for that ruse! We're New Yorkers, we're not going to give our baggage to just anyone! Instead, we went inside to the TWA check-in counter and waited on the line as the clock ticked closer and closer to our departure time.

When it was finally our turn, I smiled at the pretty girl behind the counter and pointed to the guy outside the terminal. "I'll bet those people giving that guy their luggage are gonna be in for a big surprise, right?" She looked at me like I had two heads and handed me my boarding pass, saying, "Why would that be? He works for TWA. You better hurry, your flight will be boarding soon. Have a great trip!"

Sheesh.

Rushing through a pretty weak security checkpoint, the guard with the magic wand gave us a quick once over and waived us through. Once in the waiting area, we settled into a couple of seats and did some people watching. A young couple our age, sitting not too far away, were obviously baseball fans. She was wearing a San Francisco Giants baseball hat with a ponytail protruding from the back. He sported an orange and black Giants T-Shirt. They were obviously non-New Yorkers because they both got up at the same time and left their bag unattended for a few minutes.

She hurried back and confronted her boyfriend, "I thought

YOU had the bag," before laughing at their faux pas. Any true New Yorker would have said, "What are you—an idiot? How could you leave the God-damned bag alone?"

As I fidgeted in the uncomfortable blizzard white plastic chairs, the bright red, pseudo leather backing pads provided little relief. I was still a little nervous about getting on that airplane. Slinking off into the bathroom to splash some water on my face, I quietly offered myself some encouragement, "There's no backing out now. Get yourself together, you can do this."

Getting back to our seats, Bruce remarked that I looked like I just saw a ghost. He reiterated what he had been telling us all along. "It's like riding a bus, Disco," he said. "Just follow my lead. I'm a professional." And then he smiled that sly, Eddie Haskell devilish smile. "Besides," he continued, "What could possibly go wrong?"

The calm and cool Catman was no help, either. "Just think of the chicks," he said, flashing his best Cheshire Cat smile and pointing. "Look at those blondes over there. California is loaded with blondes."

"You think the carpet matches the drapes?" Mr. B asked.

"Who cares?" smirked the Catman. That's why he's The Catman.

Regardless of their expert advice, I was still a little apprehensive. Making my way down the long walkway into the plane for the first time was a bit intimidating. You try not to think about relinquishing all control of your destiny to a stranger, but it remains in the back of your mind. For the next six hours, you are strapped inside a metal tube filled with jet fuel, hurtling over 400 mph about 30,000 feet above the ground. And you have zero control over what is about to happen. Zero.

A cute stewardess with a name tag identifying her as "Mary" greeted us at the tiny portal entrance, along with the pilot and co-pilot. "Welcome to TWA," she chirped with more than a hint of a southern accent. "Have a great flight!" I looked at the pilots and said, "Don't worry about me, I hope you guys have a great flight."

With only two seats on each side of the aisle, I couldn't believe how big the inside was. It was almost luxurious. Then I found out we were walking through First-Class without stopping. What a bummer. Passing through a set of curtains separating the riffraff in Coach from First Class was a disappointment. We had to squeeze down the aisle and find our seats in row 10. "Mr. Professional Flyer" took the window seat while I sat in the middle, leaving the aisle seat for The Catman. He wanted to get a good look at every girl's ass that walked down the aisle.

As we taxied to the runway, all I could think about was what Peach had told me the night before—"It's the takeoffs and landings that'll kill ya!" The engines, which were humming at a moderate decibel level, suddenly kicked into high gear, hurtling us down the runway at a remarkably high rate of speed. Unlike cars, planes apparently aren't equipped with shock absorbers to soften the ride on the ground. Knowing airport runways run out of room eventually, I was unsure of the protocol if we reached the end. Instead of looking out the windows, I closed my eyes.

With a massive roar of its engines, the bumpy ride gave way, and the ground below began to recede. We were airborne. Looking out the window to my left, I saw the roofs of houses, then entire neighborhoods. Soon, the skyline of Manhattan was visible out the other side, and it looked like a scale model, with a camera panning away from it. We were rising rapidly with no turning back.

At some point, we leveled out and were above the clouds. None of us spoke at first, but we were smiling from ear to ear. California, here we come!

An announcement from the flight crew indicated that lunch would be served about half-way through the flight, but no alcoholic beverages before noon.

"High noon," Mr. B commented. "I wish we were high…"

The view from above the clouds was transcendent, almost bordering on a religious experience. I just wish I could get my mother's concerns about aerodynamics out of my mind. How DOES this thing stay in the air?

After a while, with all eyes on my watch, we counted down the final seconds, "Three, two, one…" as the clock finally struck noon. I signaled to our Southern Belle stewardess, Mary, to bring us some drinks, raising an imaginary glass to my lips and taking an imaginary sip. She pointed behind me, and I saw another stewardess walking down the aisle with a drink cart.

We were a little disappointed that they only had the small, 8 ounce cans of Budweiser. Our friend Douglas used to call them "235's" because that was how many milliliters were in the can back then (about 7.9 oz). The United States was still considering adopting the metric system, and both the ounces and milliliters were displayed on the cans. But, any port in a storm, right?

It didn't take long to finish those nips, and I was already feeling much better about the whole flying experience. Having finished perusing almost every piece of paraphernalia inserted in the seatback pockets, I opened the last magazine, and the "barf bag" fell out from between the pages. The inside was lined with a plastic coating and twisty-tie flaps on the top (like you get with a loaf of bread) to "seal" it in the event you, well, needed it. The front contained amusing, step-by-step cartoon drawings of how to "use and properly dispose" of the item. There was a scorecard grid drawn on the back for use when playing a card game. That gave me an idea.

I signaled our stewardess again, and when she arrived, she said, "Hi, hon. Would you like some more drinks?" pointing at the three "dead soldiers" on our trays.

"Ab-so-freaking-lutely!" Mr. B answered.

While she was removing the empties, I asked if she could bring us a deck of cards and a pen.

"Sure can, hon!" she cheerfully drawled. What a sweetheart!

Since I was in the middle seat, my tray table was used for the discard pile. I grabbed the barf bag and used the pen to keep score. We were in the middle of a very contentious game of Rummy 500 when the pilot's voice came over the loudspeaker and made an announcement. We needed to make an emergency landing in St. Louis.

What did he say?

The San Francisco baseball fans we saw in the terminal back at JFK were sitting just a few rows behind us. The girl asked the stewardess if there was anything wrong with the airplane. She was assured it wasn't a mechanical issue, but the co-pilot had a bad kidney stone attack, and we would need to land and get him immediate medical attention. Selfishly, my first thought was hoping we were also getting another co-pilot.

We continued with our card game, but before we began to descend below the clouds, we hit some turbulence, interrupting our smooth flight. As the plane started to shake, Bruce reached for the scoresheet.

"Fuck you, man," I said while grabbing it out of his hands, "We all know you're winning; you don't need to check the score."

He continued to reach for the scoresheet without saying a word, just grabbing at the air. I turned to look at his face and realized he wasn't interested in checking the score. He was in dire need of a place to make a quick deposit.

"Mr. Professional Flyer" then proceeded to end our card game prematurely by using the bag containing our scoresheet for its original purpose.

We were on the ground in St. Louis for almost two hours as we waited for a new co-pilot to arrive. There were still four hours between us and Los Angeles, but thanks to Mr. B, we didn't have anything to keep score on anymore.

Just like riding a bus…

# the Bathroom Surprise

JoAnne had just finished her lunch when we walked through the door of "Travel Mood" on July 5th. As the lone travel agent working that day at the Sunrise Mall in Massapequa, she had been eating at her desk. She was looking at the reflection of her face in a compact mirror, using a small tissue to remove what appeared to be the remains of lunch from her teeth.

It appeared she had enjoyed a leafy, green salad.

"Hey guys. My name is JoAnne. How can I help you?" she said, quickly dumping the tissue while absentmindedly throwing the small compact mirror into her cavernous purse. I'm sure the next time she needed it would require an extensive search. She was very professional, pleasant to look at, and on the other side of thirty.

Partially hungover from celebrating our country's independence the night before, we sat down to discuss our trip plans. Obviously infatuated with three hunks in their early 20's, she flirted with us a little while we fumbled all over ourselves, trying to act like we had done this a million times before.

Our plans were spotty, at best. We envisioned a 10-day West Coast trip in the middle of August. We wanted to fly to California for a few days, then head to Arizona and visit some friends staying in Tempe before heading back to New York. It was going to cost us $272.60 with tax each.

She reserved a car from "Dollar Rent-a-Car" and gave us a nifty $5 off coupon for being first-time customers. She was a little surprised that we only wanted hotel reservations for the first three nights in Los Angeles.

"Where are you planning to stay the other nights?" she said inquisitively.

"Wherever we want," Bruce told her, defiantly, "We're making this up as we go along!"

"How about three nights at the Best Western in Hollywood?" she offered.

We could care less about the place we were staying, so we agreed, and she gave us a TWA "Fly and Drive" open voucher. If we didn't like the looks of the hotel when we got there, we could use the voucher with any participating hotel chain, based on availability. Sounded just like what we were looking for.

She prepared our airline tickets in little booklets with carbon paper between all the pages, kind of like old-fashioned credit card receipts. Then, she carefully placed our plane tickets, along with the hotel and car vouchers, into a small, red vinyl billfold marked

"TWA Getaway Vacations," and hand-wrote our itinerary on a little piece of paper.

With my OCD kicking in, I volunteered to take possession of all our travel documents, including the individual plane tickets. I would keep everything in one place. Bruce was my friend, and Sal was my cousin, but I couldn't trust them with the tickets. Knowing those Hammerheads, someone would lose something.

We were totally set. We had a car, a place to stay, and, more importantly, we had plane tickets to get us there and back.

What could possibly go wrong?

---

Unfortunately, we hadn't planned for TWA Flight 005 to make an unscheduled emergency landing in St. Louis.

Once on the ground, we waited on the tarmac for over 90 minutes before the captain finally announced a co-pilot was on his way, prompting sarcastic cheers from the passengers. Lunch was a choice of turkey or ham and cheese sandwiches, which the flight crew served while we waited. Mr. B, fresh off upchucking his breakfast, wanted no part of lunch and opted for a bag of pretzels and a coke to settle his stomach. To keep the party going, I got a rum and coke with my turkey sandwich.

The Catman took this break in the action to saunter down the aisle where he found two blondes and struck up a conversation. Bruce was looking a little pale, but his stomach began to settle, and we got a couple of 235's when the cart came around again.

"The hair of the dog," he said as he sipped the "Nectar of the Gods." The color was beginning to return to his face.

We amused ourselves over the next few hours, enjoying the in-flight movie, *The Buddy Holly Story*. When the pilot announced we were preparing for our final descent into Los Angeles International Airport, most of the passengers cheered again. Except for the couple across the aisle. They were complaining about having to miss their connecting Hawaiian flight due to the two-hour delay. Mary, slipping into her Southern Belle persona again, assured them Customer Service would take care of their new arrangements as soon as they landed.

Without a care in the world, we disembarked from the plane into a beautiful Los Angeles afternoon. On the way to the baggage claim, we made a pit stop in the public restroom. Mr. B decided to use a stall to take a crap while Catman and I headed to the urinals. While waiting for him at the baggage claim, the conveyor belt sprang into life, and suitcases of all shapes and sizes began materializing from the back area.

Emerging from the bathroom with a spring in his step, Mr. B sported a massive smile and was looking all around, like someone was following him. "We have to get out of here right now," he said. "Look what I found in the bathroom." Undoing a few buttons and pulling back one side of his shirt slightly, he revealed what looked like a small, clear, plastic bag filled with oregano.

"I was pinching a loaf," he excitedly announced, "and when I went to grab some toilet paper, this fell out from behind the dispenser. It's a bag of freaking weed!"

Son of a gun, it certainly looked like a bag of weed.

"Are you sure," I asked hesitantly.

"It's definitely hooch," Bruce confirmed, "Or at least it smells like hooch. Guess we'll have to find out, no?"

"Why would anyone leave a bag of weed in the bathroom?" I asked.

"Maybe someone was going to try and get on the plane with it," Catman offered, "But at the last minute chickened out?"

"Or maybe it was for someone else, and they're looking for it right now!" Bruce added, "Or, maybe it's a plant in an FBI sting operation?"

I'm sure the FBI is planting small bags of weed in public bath-rooms to arrest unsuspecting travelers.

"Finders keepers," I said triumphantly! "Let's get the hell out of here!"

We grabbed our bags from the crowded baggage carousel and headed to the Dollar Rent-a-Car counter. Oh man, was this going to be a great trip! Knowing we couldn't bring any weed, we were hoping to score something while out here. We knew our friends in Arizona would have plenty—it was a way of life out there—but this was undoubtedly a pleasant surprise!

The friendly dude at the red, yellow, and blue Dollar Rent-a-Car counter confirmed our reservation on the computer and directed us to the van pickup area outside. Apparently, a courtesy van transported you to the offsite location to pick up your car.

"Do I pay for everything here?" I asked innocently, having never done this before.

"No, sir," he responded cheerfully, "This counter is for reserva-tions only. You pick up the car and sign all the paperwork at the offsite location. The van will take you right to the pickup location."

"Works for me," I said, adding the classic California goodbye, "Have a nice day!"

While standing at the designated pickup location outside the main terminal, the brisk afternoon breeze was playing havoc with Bruce and Sal's hair. I smiled when I saw the tangled mess the windy Los Angeles afternoon was causing to their hair. "Nice hats, fellows!" I cracked, happy that I was wearing a baseball hat. "Hope you packed your hairbrushes."

On the ride to Dollar Rent-a-Car, we made plans to stop at a convenience store for rolling papers and a lighter immediately. We were like a bunch of giddy teenage girls at their first sleepover. I took my place in the line leading to the counter as Bruce and Sal hung outside the little waiting area with the bags.

I immediately recognized the young couple ahead of me as the

San Francisco Giants fans from our flight. We exchanged pleas-
antries and made small talk while waiting. Karen and Glenn lived
in San Francisco and were returning from their first trip to New
York, stopping first in LA to see some friends, before continuing to
Northern California. We were still chatting about the unfortunate
co-pilot emergency when it was their turn to go to the counter. I
was secretly happy they were called by the young guy with the long
blonde hair. I was eyeing the pretty woman with the jet-black hair
next to him, who seemed to be finishing up with her customer.

When she called "Next!" I strolled up to her side of the counter.
Her long black hair was in a ponytail and was a striking contrast to
the red and yellow uniform. The company logo for "Dollar Rent-a-
Car" was stitched just above her generous, yet tightly secured left
breast. Right below the stitching was a small, rectangular name tag
sporting "Kelly." She was pushing thirty and had the same pleasant
smile everyone out here seemed to possess. "Welcome to Dollar
Rent-a-Car," she said with a smile that went for miles. "How can I
help you? Is this your first time in Los Angeles?"

I suavely handed her the rental voucher that good ole JoAnne
from Travel Mood prepared with our "Fly and Drive" package.
"Yes," I said smoothly, "This is our first time out here. We're here
for a week," I instinctively pointed to Bruce and Sal outside the
lobby window. They waved at Kelly, and she waved back. Bruce
then returned to scanning the perimeter for FBI agents.

"Oh, you boys are going to have a great time here," she said
confidently.

"I hope so," I replied, trying to match her huge smile. "We had
a little problem with our flight out here, but once we arrived, things
have been looking up!"

JoAnne from Travel Mood had recommended a mid-sized Ford
Fairmont, the largest car in our price range. We tried for a Thun-
derbird, but that wasn't available for what we were willing to spend.

Just then, the young San Francisco couple from our flight

walked past me, very dejectedly. "They gave away our car," said Glenn. "They don't have any more available, so we're going to try a different place."

"Are you kidding me?" I said. "Didn't you have a reservation?"

"We had a reservation, but because we were over two hours late, they gave it away. There's nothing they can do."

"That's bullshit, my friend," I responded. "They better still have my car, or we're going to have a problem."

"Good luck with that," Glenn said cynically while heading for the exit. "We're gonna take the van back to the airport and try Hertz and Avis."

I quickly turned my attention back to Kelly and asked a simple question, but with a little more volume and urgency, "You *DO* have a car for me, don't ya, Kelly? The gentleman at the airport counter confirmed my reservation just a few minutes ago."

"I'm checking now," she said with a touch of fear, rotating her head from the computer screen to the printout on a clipboard. With a quizzical look on her face, she reviewed the details of the voucher again and then turned back to the clipboard. Now perplexed, she turned back to me and said, "I don't see your voucher number on the printed listing of the available cars."

"What does that mean?" I asked as the euphoria of finding a full bag of weed suddenly drained from my face. "I have a voucher with today's date on it, don't I?"

"Oh wait," she said after checking again. "Here it is, it was scratched out. I'm sorry, but your car was assigned to another customer. You know, you were supposed to be here over two hours ago."

Staying as calm as I could, I explained to my new friend Kelly about our delay in St. Louis and that surely, they could find us a different car, couldn't they? We saw literally 100 vehicles in the lot.

"Monday is a hectic day for rental cars," she calmly explained, "It's our policy not to hold reservations for more than an hour or so. Every car we have is accounted for. Most of the businesspeople pick them up early in the morning, so by this time of the day, we don't have many still available. I'm sorry."

"You're sorry," I said as my voice began to rise. "That's all you have, honey? I have a voucher for a rental car, so I believe you need to find me a car."

"I'm not sure I can do that, sir."

Sir?

Suddenly I went from some kid visiting Los Angeles for the first time to a "Sir"?

I turned around and got Bruce and Sal's attention outside, signaling them the universal "jerk off" gesture with my right hand. They promptly grabbed the bags and joined me inside at the counter.

"They don't have a car for us," I announced, loud enough for everyone behind us on the line to hear.

"That's bullshit," Mr. B said even louder, turning his anger to the now frightened Kelly and pointing his finger, "You better find us a car, or we are going to make a scene."

I think we were already accomplishing that.

Other people on the line were beginning to look at us like the New York maniacs we were about to become. Some of them were starting to inch away from the counter where all the action was.

"Then what exactly CAN you do for me, Kelly?" I asked snidely.

"Let me make a phone call to see if any cars are coming back today and maybe we can turn one around quickly for you. Would that be OK?"

"Thank you, Kelly," I answered, trying not to lose my temper. "But can you do me a favor? I'd like to speak to the manager." She made a quick phone call, and after a few minutes, a nice gentleman with a name tag of "Jimmy" emerged from the door behind the counter. He seemed a little intimidated at first since Bruce was beginning to snort like a bull approaching a matador. There was smoke coming out of his ears already.

"You better find us a car, Jack," he shouted as his New York attitude was on display for all to see, putting poor Jimmy on the defensive immediately. "We have a goddam reservation, and now you're telling me you don't have a car? What's wrong with this picture?"

"There's no reason to raise your voice, sir," Jimmy offered as an olive branch to the quickly escalating situation. What Jimmy didn't know was that once Mr. B went off, there was no turning back. There was a fire in his eyes, and whether you solved his problem or not, you were going to hear from him.

"I think this is a GREAT reason to raise my voice!" he said, while turning to the murmuring crowd behind him, still waiting their turn. "I can't think of a BETTER reason to raise my voice, can you, Jimmy pal?" Little did Bruce know in just a few hours, he would have plenty of reasons to raise his voice again.

It was time to play Good Cop-Bad Cop, something that Bruce and I had perfected over the years. I stepped between him and Jimmy and tried to play the part of Henry Kissinger.

"Wait a minute, wait a minute," I said calmly, stepping in front of Mr. B and easing him behind me. "Jim, can we just try and figure out how to solve this problem? We've reserved a car, we need a car, and you must have cars available in the lot, right? Why not just give us someone else's car that's due to arrive later today?"

He explained that he couldn't do that. Other customers had already prepaid for their cars, but all we had was a reservation voucher.

Suddenly, I was making a mental note to strangle JoAnne from Travel Mood when we returned to Massapequa.

Jimmy quickly commandeered Kelly's computer and was now feverishly typing on the keyboard. I could see a small drop of sweat racing down the left side of his cheek.

He noted there was a car due back very soon, and he could have it turned around for us in about an hour. He also offered to take $15 off the full rental price (it was like getting one day for free) and give us a full tank of gas to start with.

Continuing in my "Good Cop" role, I thanked him, and we worked out the logistics. We would take the van back to the main terminal and call again in about an hour for an update.

Returning to LAX, we fruitlessly checked with some of the other rental counters. Without a paid reservation, you weren't getting a car at this hour of the day. So, we did what any other 20-something travelers would do in a foreign land, we found a bar and plotted our next move.

Dollar Rent-a-Car may have tried to burn us, but we won in the end. There was no way Jimmy wouldn't find us a car after the scene we just made in his lobby. He wanted nothing more to do with these crazy New Yorkers. Not only did he find us a car, our new friend Jimmy had it delivered to the airport so we didn't have to go back to the rental office.

Wasn't that nice of him?

A little over an hour later, we had our vehicle, a blue, 2-door, Chevy Chevette. Unfortunately, it was a compact car. We could only fit two of our suitcases inside the trunk, placing the third one in the back seat. I took the wheel, and we headed out of the airport. It was close to 5 pm now, and we were going to be heading out into Los Angeles traffic during rush hour. But we had a bag of weed and 10 days ahead of us.

Leaving the airport, we saw the young couple from San Francisco, Karen and Glenn, looking forlorn and sitting on their luggage at the curb, outside the "Arrival" gate. I assumed they were still carless.

"Wanna ask them if they need a ride?" Bruce deadpanned with a sly smile on his face.

No way we were letting LA beat us on our first day...

# the Navigation Specialist

Mr. B noticed the sign before anyone else, announcing with glee, "There it is, the 110!"

The 110?

"Are you sure about that?" I asked, "I thought we were looking for the I-10?"

"Not possible, Mr. B," the Catman confidently chimed in, "It's the I-10, not the 110. We're nowhere near the 110."

Then, I also saw the sign for Interstate 110, clear as day, not Interstate 10. Bruce was right.

"I told you, you Hammerhead," Mr. B said.

"That's not fucking possible, Catman," I yelled into the back seat, "Where the hell is Interstate 10?"

"Oh shit," the Catman injected after taking a closer look at the map, "We're going south, not north. Here's Redondo Beach, it's south of the airport. That IS the goddamn 110!"

We had been driving for 20 minutes in the wrong direction.

In retrospect, maybe we should have waited until we got to the hotel to try that weed...

After leaving the airport, we found a 7-11 connected to a gas station on West Century Avenue. We picked up some necessary supplies, including a case of beer, a bag of ice, and a Styrofoam cooler. Behind the counter, a clerk named "Dave" dug out a map of California for us that included street-level detail for Los Angeles, San Diego, and San Francisco. It was neatly folded into the traditional 8-inch x 4-inch rectangle. But once opened, it expanded to cover the entire hood of the car. The trick was trying to refold it back to its original state and stash it in the glove compartment. Good luck with that.

The 7-11 anchored a small strip mall that also included a liquor store, a nail salon, a deli, and a tiny head shop. After packing the cooler with the beer and ice, we left the car outside the 7-11 and made our way to the head shop to pick up rolling papers, a couple of lighters, and a small pipe.

Armed with our trusty "Fly and Drive" voucher that JoAnne from Travel Mood had so nicely prepared for us, we sat in the car to get things organized before attempting to make our way to the Best Western on South Sepulveda Boulevard. While twisting the radio dial to find a rock station, we came upon one that was playing Bruce Springsteen's "Born to Run."

"I have an idea," Bruce said with that mischievous twinkle in his eye, "Every time we hear a Bruce song, we have to smoke."

"Every time?" I asked.

"Every time," he answered.

"No matter the situation?" I countered.

"No matter the situation," he repeated back to me.

I glanced at Catman in the back. "Don't look at me," he said. "I'm not committing to that." We loved the Catman, but he wasn't that much of a smoker, to begin with.

"Let's do it, man," I said to Bruce as I grabbed his pinky with mine, and a pact was made. The "Springsteen Burn" was now official. Mr. B packed the bowl with our newfound weed and lit the fuse. We were officially on our way.

For those of you keeping score at home, the weed Bruce found in the bathroom of LAX was excellent.

As the final strains of "Born to Run" faded, Mr. B, who was sitting in the shotgun seat, opened the map, trying to find our hotel. The sheer size of it was intimidating as it now occupied most of the space in the front seat. JoAnne from Travel Mood had prepared our voucher with a confirmation number and the hotel address. We were looking for the Best Western off South Sepulveda Boulevard, in Los Angeles.

It didn't take long for things to spiral out of control.

"I can't figure this shit out at all," Bruce said after looking over the map for a few minutes. "There's a 110, an I-10, a 105, and a 405. Wait, there's two freakin' South Sepulveda Boulevards – how the fuck can that be true? This is bullshit, man."

As captain of this ship, I acted expeditiously and relieved Mr. B of his navigational duties on the spot, promoting the Catman to "Navigational Specialist," First Class. Mr. B, taking the demotion like the professional he was, crumpled the huge map into a small ball, throwing it into the general direction of our new navigator.

"We need to figure out where we are before we can get to where we need to be," the Catman said intelligently with a calming voice. After all, he was the only one in the vehicle that wasn't currently stoned. "Let's go back to the 7-11 guy and figure this out."

Bruce and I stumbled out of the car as most of the remaining smoke escaped in a mushroom cloud. Catman was going to have to do most of the talking. Making our way back inside, we approached our good buddy Dave, who sold us the map.

"You guys again, eh?" he said through a big smile. Not sure if the marijuana was making me paranoid, but I got the feeling he knew we were stoned. The car was only about 100 feet from his window, in broad daylight, so chances are he saw the cloud of smoke when we got out.

Catman explained our predicament to Dave, and he seemed familiar with where the Best Western was located, but it wasn't in the best neighborhood. "That's in West LA near Rancho Park, off I-10," he said. "Kind of a shithole, but not as bad as East LA," he added, noting that it was about 15 miles north of the airport.

Trying to flatten our trusty California map, which was currently in the shape of a ball instead of a neat rectangle, Catman laid it out on the grimy countertop and used the palm of his hand like he was ironing a shirt. He asked Dave to point out where we needed to go. Dave traced our route on the map with his finger, moving from Aviation Boulevard straight onto Interstate 105, which connects with Interstate 405 going north. I-10 is right off the 405. Easy Peasy.

"You're going to run into a bunch of cloverleafs," Jimmy warned as he expertly folded the map back into its original 4" by 8" rectangle and handed it back to the Catman. "Just follow the signs. You can't miss it." Then he flashed a slow, devilish smile, not unlike "The Grinch" from the Dr. Seuss books.

A slight chill went down my spine, and suddenly I was a little suspicious of good ole' Dave.

As New Yorkers, we could easily navigate roads, right? Except, this was like nothing we've ever seen before. The cloverleaf intersections of the 105 and the 405 are like no others in the world. Even if we were stone-cold sober, this would have been a problem for us. Unfortunately, we were far from stone-cold sober.

"Do you think he knew we were stoned?" I asked Mr. B as we got back to the car.

"Of course, he knew we were stoned," he laughed. "You have a little red light flashing over the top of your head, blinking, 'stoned … stoned … stoned!'"

I gave him the finger and started the car.

The Catman took control of the navigation, barking orders from the back seat. As instructed, we headed down Aviation Boulevard and, just like Dave indicated, ran right into the 105. Unfortunately, he failed to mention that you can't get onto the 105 from Aviation Boulevard because the 105 was elevated and ran over it. There was no entrance or exit ramps from Aviation Boulevard.

Crap.

Now I was certain Dave was fucking with us because he knew we were high.

Springing into action, our new Navigation Specialist, First Class, directed us to follow Imperial Highway, which ran parallel to the 105. Imperial Highway intersected with the 405 just ahead. We could see the 405 now, and Mr. B exchanged a high-five with the Catman. Of course, as we approached the massive cloverleaf for the 8-lane 405, none of the entrance ramps connected with Imperial Highway, and we drove right under, and then past, the 405.

Damn that evil, twisted Dave!

It took some luck (and another set of beers), but we finally found the 105 and approached the giant cloverleaf for the 405 again. I obediently followed the signs for the North entrance, and we were finally on our way…

---

We ran into some traffic around the exit for Redondo Beach, but things started to ease after that. We had been traveling for about 20 minutes when Bruce first noticed that sign for the 110, which meant we were going in the wrong direction.

"What the fuck, Catman, I thought you were navigating?" Mr. B said.

"I am navigating," Catman insisted, "But I'm not driving. Disco, you must have taken the 405 south instead of north, you dickweed. We've been heading south ever since."

"Well," I said, trying to maintain order in the face of chaos, "What do we do now, Magellan? How do we get to the I-10?"

"Take the 110 north," he said, gazing at the map, "That takes us all the way to I-10. No more exits."

Mr. B had enough, cracking open a cold Coors and firing up a bowl. "I think we need to take a break with the pause that refreshes." And he was right.

It took about a half hour, but we finally made it to the I-10 and were heading to the Best Western. It was almost 7:30 pm LA time. I was looking forward to getting into our room and crashing.

Pulling into the Best Western, we congratulated ourselves for finally making it. "I'll go inside and get the keys," I said, stepping out of the car a little shaky, but no worse for wear. What should have been a 20-minute trip from the airport turned into two hours from hell. But we were here now, and soon, all would be right with the world once again.

Yeah, right.

Mr. B and the Catman went to search for one of those luggage valets' carts for our stuff. Wearily, but confidently, I moseyed up to the registration desk, handing "Kenny" our Travel Mood voucher. He wore a neatly pressed spicy mustard brown shirt with the Best Western crown logo stitched in black directly on the shirt pocket. His contrasting red tie was slightly askew as if he had been wearing it all day long. I regaled him with our nightmare on the 405.

"That happens a lot out here," he assured me, running his free hand through his wavy blonde hair to clear it from his eyes. He had the look of a weekend surfer dude. "You really have to be familiar with the roads, or you can get lost fairly easily."

No shit, Sherlock.

He looked at the voucher a little quizzically, then placed it back onto the counter, facing me, to point out something. I leaned in to get a better look.

"This confirmation number isn't for this Best Western," he said, pulling a pen from his breast pocket and circling the number for clarification. "This number starts with the letters 'WH.' Our confirmation numbers start with 'WL' for West LA. 'WH' is for the Best Western in West Hollywood."

I was stunned into silence, opening my mouth but not able to speak. Sensing my dismay, Kenny offered, "It's not far from here, only about 15 minutes or so."

I dejectedly walked into the lobby and found Mr. B and the Catman hanging out with a loaded luggage valet and informed them of our situation. Although it didn't go over too well, we avoided a scene and put everything back into the car and headed to West Hollywood.

No sense in arguing with Kenny, this had nothing to do with him. We were just in the wrong place.

Apparently, our good buddy, JoAnne from Travel Mood, had written the wrong address for our Best Western on the voucher. We are going to have a very long talk with that chick when we get back.

Before leaving for West Hollywood, Catman retrieved the map from the car and went back to the reservation desk to plot out the best route with Kenny. Bruce and I waited for him outside.

"Can you believe this shit?" I said to him while we were sipping on a couple of beers. "How did all our plans go to shit so quickly?"

"Who cares?" he shot back. Frankly, I thought he would be more upset after the scene he made at Dollar Rent-a-Car. Maybe he was mellow because of the weed?

"We're in fucking California, man!" he waxed poetically, "We're on the left coast, and everywhere you look are blonde chicks. This place isn't going to burn us. We're from New York, nobody can burn us!"

I couldn't argue about that.

We raised our beers to toast our newfound attitude. We were going to win every battle while we were out in California, or we were going to die trying.

Catman returned with a big smile on his face. "This other place is so much cooler," he said. "It's in the center of Hollywood, fer Christ's sake. Everything is within a mile or so of our hotel. There are a million bars and clubs, not to mention Hollywood Boulevard and all those famous streets."

And just like that, we decided to let JoAnne from Travel Mood off the hook and send her a Christmas Card this December!

# the Plush Horse Inn

Santa Monica Boulevard would take us directly into West Hollywood. Our Best Western was about 12 miles to the east. It didn't take long for the riff-raff of West LA to dissipate in the rear-view mirror. Soon, new, and more modern-looking architecture was replacing rundown businesses and seedy looking restaurants.

It was approaching 8 pm, but there was still plenty of light left when Mr. B shouted, "Holy Shit, we're in Beverly Hills!" We were suddenly surrounded by chic boutiques and pristine storefronts. Even the streets and sidewalks looked cleaner.

Many California roads, like Santa Monica Boulevard, displayed the names of the cross streets above the traffic lights, spanning the lanes of traffic. The bright green signs were adorned with white letters and illuminated at night, allowing drivers to see the street names from a distance as they approached an intersection.

Like kids in the back seat of their father's station wagon, we were announcing the names of the familiar, iconic streets we'd seen on TV or in the movies. We passed intersections for Wilshire Boulevard and Rodeo Drive before stopping at the light for North Beverly Drive. Just then, Catman looked down North Beverly and yelled, "Disco, it's the Beverly Hillbillies street!"

We all turned at once, and sure enough, the street was easily recognizable, lined with palm trees, just like we'd seen a hundred times on TV. I made a U-Turn at the next light and turned up North Beverly Drive, just like the Clampetts did. The two-lane street was lined with palm trees, alternating from short with thick trunks to tall and skinny trunks. The neatly manicured lawns and shrubbery were a sight to behold. It was impossible to drive up this street without hearing that sharp baritone voice telling us the story of a man named "Jed." I can still hear that dueling banjo-picking music in my head.

As if on cue, Mr. B started singing, "Come and listen to my story 'bout a man named Jed…" and before you knew it, we were all singing along.

After taking that quick detour and consulting our trusty map, we were only a few miles from the Best Western, so we stopped at a McDonald's for a few burgers. We didn't have much left in the tank, and our bodies were still operating on New York time. Factor in not much sleep from the night before, and all the excitement so far today, we just wanted to get to our room and recharge for tomorrow.

We quickly located North Highland Avenue and made our final turn before getting to the hotel, now traveling through the heart of Hollywood and the tourist district. Places like "Grauman's Chinese Theatre" and the stars on the "Walk of Fame" were walking distance from the Best Western. We were right in the heart of the action.

Thanks, JoAnne, from Travel Mood!

This Best Western was the Taj Mahal compared to the dump we mistakenly went to in West LA. A beautiful covered entranceway greeted us as we made our way to the front office. Instead of going directly inside, Catman suggested we take a quick tour around the property. I veered away from the main entrance and drove through the packed parking lot. The hotel sported two floors, and all the rooms had balconies with chairs and small tables.

As we circled around the property, we saw it was shaped like a "U," with rooms on both sides protecting an open courtyard in the middle. Privacy bushes prevented us from getting a good look at the courtyard, but you could easily make out the tops of yellow and red-colored umbrellas, all sporting the Best Western crown logo. "They have a pool, man!" the Catman exclaimed. "Pools mean chicks. Chicks and pools mean bathing suits. Bathing suits mean bikinis!"

Entering the lobby, we separated into different areas. The sizable decorative clock in the lobby was built right into the stone wall above the fireplace. The hands were free-floating between four dots instead of the traditional 12 numbers, representing 12, 3, 6, and 9. If I had to guess, it was a little after nine when I headed to the reservation desk. Mr. B spied a luggage cart on the other side of the lobby and went in that direction.

"I'm going to grab that before some other poor schmuck can get to it," he said with his voice trailing off the further away he got.

The Catman simply headed down the hallway on a mission, "I'm gonna find that pool."

While Mr. B and the Catman went their separate ways, I dragged my weary ass to the counter and encountered a blonde (what else?) named Caroline. She was wearing that same spicy brown mustard-colored shirt our friend Kenny from the Best Western in West LA wore, but her rack caused the crown logo to stretch ever so slightly. After cheerfully taking my voucher, she made a few keystrokes on the computer keyboard and politely told me that they had given away our room.

Come again?

"I'm sorry, we can only hold your reservation until 6 pm unless you are prepaid or called us if you are being delayed. Unfortunately, we're very booked and gave your room to another customer about an hour ago."

Weren't we at the other Best Western about an hour ago?

I understood the issue we had at Dollar Rent-a-Car because we only had a reservation. But we pre-paid for this open-ended voucher.

"Caroline," I said very nicely, informing her I have a pre-paid, open-ended voucher. "Why would you give away a room that has already been paid for?"

"We can only hold rooms after 6 pm with a prepaid voucher," she said as she continued to smile, "That's not prepaid, it's pre-approved and authorized by Master Card, but it's not a payment voucher. Your credit card has not yet been charged. Since it's open-ended, you could have decided to stay at any one of the participating hotels, so we reserve the right to cancel the reservation if we don't hear from you by 6 pm."

Cross JoAnne from Travel Mood off my Christmas Card list.

"When it's busy like this," Caroline continued, "We sometimes grant customer requests for an additional room. I'm so sorry. Many times, customers with additional family members or grown children will ask for a second room once they get here. We always tell them we have to wait until after 6 pm, and then we might be able to accommodate them."

Well, isn't that special?

"Let me get this straight," I said, suppressing my quietly building rage. "You gave our room to someone who already had a room and wanted another one?"

"I didn't say that, sir. I said we sometimes do that."

"Well, listen, Caroline. Do you think that, sometimes, people don't know about your stupid fucking 6 pm policy? Do you sometimes think of that? Is it possible that, just sometimes, when you give away someone's reserved room that they don't have any other place to fucking stay?"

Of course, obscenities always seem to bring out the manager from the back room. "Is there a problem here?" said the guy wearing the "Gregory" name tag.

"You tell me?" I deadpanned back to him. "It seems you have given away our room and now we don't have any place to stay. To me, that sounds like a fucking problem."

"There's no need for profanity, sir," he said as he turned to Caroline to ask what happened. After a brief update of the situation, he got a little nervous and said, "Unfortunately, we don't have any rooms at this time. Would you like me to check if we have any rooms available tomorrow?"

Sal was now walking into the lobby after checking out the pool. I couldn't bring myself to get the words out of my mouth.

"What's wrong?" Catman asked as his Cheshire Cat smile disappeared from his face.

"They gave our room away, the Mother Fuckers. We should have called when we were at the other place, goddamn it."

"This is not going to go over well with Mr. B," he said, stating the obvious.

In a much calmer, almost defeated tone, I asked Gregory to please call the other Best Western and see if they had a room there. Of course, they were also booked. I wonder if he talked to our pal, Kenny?

"Can I make a suggestion," little Caroline said sheepishly, trying to not make matters worse. "Since TWA caused the delay, maybe they can help you find a room? There are usually more vacancies near the airport, you know."

Just then, Mr. B entered the lobby with the luggage cart filled with our stuff. He took one look at the scene unfolding at the registration desk and asked, "What's going on? Did I miss something?"

"We're leaving. They gave away our room."

It took a few minutes, but we dragged Mr. B out of the lobby before he got us all arrested. We slowly put everything back into the car again and headed back to the airport.

"Let's just get another place," a defeated Catman said. "There's got to be plenty of places we can stay in. Look at all these hotels."

"No fucking way," I said. "We've come too far to give in now. We are going back to that freaking airport, and I am going to get someone at TWA to get us a hotel, end of story."

The drive back to the airport was mostly quiet. Although we were exhausted and beaten up, we weren't going to give up. Mr. B had calmed down a little but was silently fuming. The Catman was sitting in the backseat with his eyes closed, catching a few zzz's.

It was after 10 pm when we parked in the short-term parking lot and dragged our weary asses into the TWA terminal to find Customer Service. Once again, I did most of the talking.

"Good evening, sir," said another in a long line of blonde women we have encountered in just a few short hours in Los Angeles. Her name tag said, "Sherry." She was a lot more mature than the other people we had encountered during this disaster of a first day. "How may I help you?"

Instead of sitting on the sidelines, Mr. B and the Catman joined me at the counter. We thought we had more strength in numbers.

I gave her the Reader's Digest version of our plight and all the events that led us to this point in time. I then gave her my best impression of a cool, calm, and collected human being I could muster, hoping to get on her good side. After all, she was about the same age as my mother, and I was hoping she might have pity on our souls like she would her own adult children.

"May I call you Sherry?" I politely asked, receiving a nod of approval in return. "Sherry, it would be greatly appreciated if you could assist us in finding lodging for a few nights as we feel this entire mess was the result of a delay caused by your airline. We could really use your help."

"I'm so sorry, boys," she said with soulful eyes and tilting her head. I got the feeling this "pouring on the charm" stuff might just work. My mother always said you can catch more flies with honey than you can with vinegar, and I thought we had Sherry right where we wanted her.

"However, there isn't anything I can do for you," she reported before issuing a sincere apology, "I'm so sorry."

So much for honey instead of vinegar.

"Unless the delay caused you to miss a connecting flight," she continued, "there's not too much I can do."

"Well, what can you do, Grandma?" Mr. B growled. Oh jeez, that wasn't going to help at all. "You better go find someone who *CAN* do something, or there is going to be a real problem here," he promised. I could see the fear in Sherry's eyes as she picked up the phone and paged for "Mr. Lobeck" to come to the Customer Service desk.

Morphing again into our best "Good Cop-Bad Cop" roles, I turned to the quietly raging Mr. Bruce and asked him to please be more respectful of Sherry. "She's trying to help us, man."

"She's not trying hard enough!" he said as the Catman led him away from the counter and over to the rows of seats near the windows.

"I'm so sorry, Sherry," I said, turning back to the counter. "It's been a long, hard day, and we are a little on edge. I apologize for my friend's unnecessary outburst."

I was laying it on thick now.

"There was no call for that. I'm sure you are doing everything in your power to help us find a place to stay."

"Thank you so much. I'm sorry, I don't even know your name?"

"You can just call me Paul, ma'am."

I had her back where I needed her to be. This "Good Cop-Bad Cop" thing works well. She was no longer helping a customer; she was trying to find a room for her little boy and his friends.

After clicking away at the computer keyboard for a few seconds, the printer behind her awoke and was banging out information one line at a time. She grabbed the printed sheet and tore it at the perforation, studying it as she walked back to the counter. We were still waiting for Mr. Lobeck to show up when she said, "Let me make a quick phone call." She was speaking to someone on the phone when Mr. Lobeck showed up. His hair was slightly tousled, and my first thought was Sherry woke him up from a nap.

"Can I help you, sir," he said as he walked behind the counter, standing next to Sherry. Unlike Sherry, who was wearing a casual red TWA collared shirt, he was wearing a button-down white shirt under a nicely tailored black sports jacket, donning a neatly knotted red tie bearing the TWA logo. He had dark-rimmed glasses like Gary Busey wore in *The Buddy Holly Story* we saw on the flight from St. Louis to LA. From the side, I heard Mr. B yell out, "You better help!"

This man must have been a bigwig because his name tag only said "Mr. Lobeck" with no first name. I was about to launch into another summary of our sad story when Sherry hung up the phone and offered her version.

When she finished, she added a new twist. "Also, Mr. Lobeck, I was able to find them accommodations at the Plush Horse Inn. It's only about 20 minutes from here."

'That's wonderful news, Sherry!" I said before turning to Mr. Lobeck, "You guys are going to pick up the tab, right, since this was all your fault?"

"Who said anything about picking up the tab?" he asked.

"Why wouldn't you? We lost a room in the middle of Hollywood because of your airline. Now, we're being relocated to a place near the airport. The least you could do is pay for our hotel."

"Sir," he said with authority, "TWA is without question responsible for the two-hour delay on your arrival into Los Angeles. However, they certainly aren't responsible for a hotel not holding your room because it took you over six hours from arriving in Los Angeles to get to their property, which is only about 20 miles from here."

If we were playing chess, the next word out of his mouth would have been, "Check."

This line of reasoning might have worked with weary travelers from other parts of the country, but we were from New York. Bruce and I had made a pact to not go quietly into the night without making a big fuss.

"Mr. Lobeck," I offered in a quiet tone, sounding a little like Perry Mason speaking to a jury, "Don't you think that TWA is somewhat responsible for the events of today?"

I then turned and looked directly at Sherry, who I suspected was on the verge of tears.

"Sherry has gone out of her way to find us a place to stay. Maybe it's time that you stepped up to the plate and did your best to ensure that we will continue to choose TWA. After all, don't you want to be remembered for helping us out in our time of need?"

Mr. Lobeck looked at our now useless hotel voucher and made us an offer we couldn't refuse. TWA would pay for two of the three nights (it was $37.00 per night) and issue a voucher for breakfast the next morning at the hotel.

Checkmate.

I thanked him profusely, grabbed the vouchers, and we headed out to the Plush Horse Inn, which was at 1700 Pacific Coast Highway off Palos Verdes Boulevard, south of Redondo Beach and near Torrance Beach. We passed this area about five hours ago when we were going in the wrong direction on the 405. Now it was the right direction.

It was past midnight by the time we got there, which translated to 3 am New York time.

I gathered several colorful tourist brochures from the lobby before we headed up to our room. We had a couple of days in LA and wanted to take advantage of some of the attractions.

California tried to burn us on our first day, but our "Never take no for an answer" New York attitude made sure we had a rental car. On top of that, now we had two free nights in a hotel, including a complimentary breakfast tomorrow. So, who burned who?

And boy, were we going to make the most of that free breakfast…

# the Guy from Tickets Galore!

TWA had provided us with an open voucher for a free breakfast, so we took full advantage. We only had one shot at this, and we were going to make the most of it. Our breakfast order could have fed eight people.

Catman took charge when we first woke up, grabbing the room

service menu and positioning himself at the tiny desk in the corner. He found a small pad in the desk drawer with the Plush Horse Inn logo on it and a 'Bic' pen with black ink.

"Let's make this count, boys," he said as he started calling out the available breakfast items and making notes on the pad. "There are pancakes, French Toast, eggs, fruit platters, assorted Danish, you name it, looks like they have it. What'll it be?"

"All of it," Mr. B said as he slowly rolled off the couch into a sitting position. "Let's make those fuckers pay for this!"

"I want pancakes and French Toast with sausage and bacon," I said, placing my order. "You know what? How about some hash browns to go with that, too?"

At first, Mr. B was going to order a giant "Hungry Man" omelet. Then the Catman found something better and shouted, "What about the "steak and eggs" platter?"

That was all Mr. B had to hear. He ordered both.

After about fifteen minutes of contemplation, we came up with the following order:

- 2 steak and egg platters
- 1 Hungry Man Omelet (with four eggs)
- 1 Pancake stack with bacon and sausage
- 1 French Toast platter with bacon and sausage
- 1 fruit platter
- 1 Danish platter
- 2 pots of coffee
- 2 carafes of orange juice

The total cost in 1978 was $22.95. Adjusted for inflation in 2020 would be about $120.00.

It took almost an hour for the feast to arrive. We attacked it like we were on death row and headed to The Chair. When the dust settled, we could barely move. The carnage was everywhere. The room looked like there was a food fight. Well, what else are you going to do with little Danishes that look like frisbees?

---

I encountered Richie from "Tickets Galore!" after gorging on our free breakfast from TWA. He was operating a kiosk in the lobby of the Plush Horse Inn. The booth had a large, green sign with a splash of yellow and the words, "See me about tickets!" in bright red letters. He was a tall, thin guy wearing a green T-shirt mimicking the sign's color scheme with the "Tickets Galore!" logo on the front, proudly displaying a "Richie" name tag. There was a red sweater tied around his waist, and he had long, streaky blonde hair split down the middle of his head. If you saw him from the back, you would have sworn he was a chick.

"Hellloooo, my friend!" he greeted me in a high-pitched voice as I approached the booth. "You staying here at The Plush?" He was a little over-the-top friendly for me, especially at ten in the morning. "What can I do for you this beautiful Los Angeles morning?"

We talked about securing tickets for Disney and Universal and the advantages of buying discounted tickets from "Tickets Galore!" Besides the price difference, purchasing tickets now would help us avoid the lines at the parks. As he spoke, I tried not to stare at his face too long. I was sure he was wearing mascara and eyeliner.

He suggested we take the Universal Studios tour and get a 2-day pass for Disneyland because it was only a few miles from "The Plush," as he continued to call it. We talked about other things to do while in LA, and he asked if we were planning to see a taping of *The Tonight Show*.

"Do you sell tickets for that?" I immediately asked.

"Oh no, my friend!" he laughed. "Those tickets are free, but you can only get them from the studio in Burbank. You should take the NBC Studio tour, that's a fun couple of hours. I have tickets for the tour, but not *The Tonight Show* itself."

The two-hour tour of the complex in Burbank got you inside the studio where they tape *The Tonight Show with Johnny Carson*. He informed us that since the tickets to see a taping of Carson were complimentary, they were hard to come by. "People sleep out the night before," he said, "so you have to be willing to sacrifice."

Bruce and I had slept out several times to get tickets to hockey playoff games and concerts, so it wasn't new to us. You do what you have to, you know? To us, it was a labor of love. In our small circle of friends, if we didn't make the sacrifice of sleeping out for tickets, nobody else would.

This was a must-see for me, as a television junkie. There would be no greater triumph than to see a taping of *The Tonight Show* while out in California. It wouldn't take much convincing for Bruce and Sal. I bought tickets for the 11 am NBC Studio Tour on Thursday.

Richie then prepared all the tickets and included the colorful tourist brochures that contained the necessary information, including park times and directions. "You guys are going to have a FABULOUS time!" he said in a sing-song kind of way, spending way too long on the word, "fabulous!" He was smiling and showing his beautiful teeth as he handed me the package.

Our last night at "The Plush" was tomorrow (Wednesday). We planned on driving to San Diego for the weekend, so we still needed a place to stay until then. Learning from our previous experiences, I reserved two more nights at "The Plush" just to be safe.

---

Following Richie's advice, we spent an entire day in Hollywood, including taking the Universal Studios tour. A motorized tram took us through the backlots where they filmed movies and TV shows. We got to see the sets used on some of our favorite movies, like Norman Bates' house in *Psycho* and where they filmed scenes from *Jaws*.

Universal had both rides and attractions based on their popular movies. At one point, we were stranded underground in a replica of the San Francisco "Bay Area Rapid Transit" (BART) subway car during a scene from the movie *Earthquake*. Then, we were almost eaten by the shark from *Jaws* as our boat toured Amity Island. While I was taking pictures of all the exciting surroundings and iconic scenes, the Catman was taking pictures almost exclusively of all the beautiful women.

His pictures were much more interesting than mine.

It turned out that Universal Studios was near Burbank. Since it closed at 6 pm in those days, we decided to do some recon after leaving the park to locate NBC. We found the studio off West Alameda Avenue and drove around the complex a few times. There was a little park just a block away from the studio and a small motel called The Baja within a few hundred yards of the studio entrance.

"We should stay right here," Mr. B suggested as we circled and passed The Baha a second time. "They have a pool. We can check in on Thursday morning before we do the tour."

It sounded like a great idea, except I didn't want to wait until Thursday morning and take a chance they no longer had any vacancies.

"Let's go reserve a room right now," I suggested, pulling into the parking lot.

"Didn't you just add two more days to our stay at 'The Plush'?" the Catman reminded me.

I guess we're calling it "The Plush" from now on, thanks to Richie.

"No biggie," I said. "We can cancel that when we get back. Let's see if they have any rooms for Thursday and Friday."

Apparently, they had plenty of vacancies since the parking lot was only half full. Even though it was so close to the NBC studio, I doubted any of Carson's celebrity guests were staying here.

Using my credit card, I reserved a room for both nights. Our new plan was to stay at The Baja on Thursday night, then go to the ticket line about 3 am, and get tickets for Friday's show.

After seeing the show on Friday (it taped around 5:30 pm), we would crash at The Baja for the night and head out to San Diego early Saturday morning, spending the weekend there.

Now that we actually had a plan in place for the next few days, we headed into Downtown Hollywood to get something to eat and check out the nightlife. The Catman immediately recognized the area and pointed to a familiar place just up ahead. "Hey, isn't that the Best Western that screwed us?"

"It sure is, those fuckers," I said.

Mr. B then shouted from the backseat, "It IS them! Look!!! That's the counter chick, and she's with a guy who looks like that dickhead manager! They're standing outside the lobby, smoking a cigarette! Disco, we have to do a drive-by!!!"

I obediently turned into the driveway and headed to the lobby entrance. Mr. B dropped his drawers and stuck his ass out the backseat window. We drove right by them with a full moon on display, beeping the horn and giving them the finger.

Of course, it wasn't them.

Just a couple of people who, a few seconds ago, were enjoying a peaceful cigarette break.

Realizing we hadn't eaten since the enormous breakfast feast, we stopped at a pizza place that had a sign in the window touting "New York Style Pizza!" It was only New York-style pizza if they had dropped it in the middle of a subway station and had the homeless urinate on it. It was just awful.

Thank goodness for that free breakfast.

It was starting to get dark when we left the pizza place and strolled the Hollywood "Walk of Fame" to see the famous people honored with "Stars" embedded in the concrete walks. Across the street was Grauman's Chinese Theatre, where celebrities' signatures along with their hand and footprints are preserved forever in concrete.

We stopped in a bar to have a couple of beers, but after a few minutes realized there were no women inside. We were surrounded by men that seemed to be looking at us as fresh meat. The Catman got the vibe almost immediately.

"This is a mistake," he said, "Most of these guys are prettier than us."

"You're crazy," I said. "It's early, man. Give it a chance. Look, they have a pool table!" I put a quarter on the edge of the table so we would play the next game.

Mr. B, who had disappeared to the bathroom, came back with a frightened look in his eyes. "We have to get out of here right now," he said in a low voice, pointing to a sign on the wall near the pool table, "It's a fucking gay bar."

The sign had "GAY STREET" in big, white letters.

Finishing our beers in just a few gulps, we slunk out of there, practically running to our car. Our Navigator First Class, the Catman, found that we were close to the famous "Hollywood" sign, and since night had already come, we drove around trying to find it.

Considering it is one of the most significant landmarks in Hollywood, and lit up like a Christmas Tree, we never found it.

Anyone know where I could find a competent navigator?

It turns out, we were on the wrong side of the sign. We did, however, manage to get lost in the Hollywood Hills, ironically while the radio DJ was playing Bob Seger's "Hollywood Nights." We found a little park bench between the multi-million-dollar mansions with a great view of Hollywood glowing below and were able to pause and reflect on that wondrous sight.

It was the first time we had a chance to relax and reflect. We were almost 3,000 miles from home and totally on our own.

Thanks to our good pal Richie and "Tickets Galore!," we were heading to Disneyland tomorrow and going to see a taping of *The Tonight Show* on Friday night.

Life is good…

---

The three of us previously made a pilgrimage to Orlando's Disney World in January of 1977 with two other friends, Keith and Eggy, in my 1975 Chevy Nova. As advertised, it was the most magical place on Earth. Although back then, that was all they had to offer in the way of theme parks in Orlando.

US 192, which today resembles a tourist attraction itself, was a deserted road back in 1977. It wasn't littered with hotels, theme restaurants, and roadside attractions. It was a few miles of nothing.

Central Florida had some tourist attractions, like the Alligator Farm in Kissimmee, but Disney was what people came for. There was no EPCOT, MGM Studios, or the Animal Kingdom. Only the Magic Kingdom.

We spent two days touring Disney World and going on all the rides and attractions, but also spent a lot of time chasing the pretty girls dressed as "Alice in Wonderland," "Cinderella," and "Sleeping Beauty." They were the only female costumed characters who revealed their faces and figures.

The Catman tried, unsuccessfully, to get a date with Alice in Wonderland, but as you know, the characters aren't allowed to speak to the guests. That didn't stop us, or the Catman, from pursuing her all over the Magic Kingdom. Wherever she appeared, we were right there. You could call it a form of stalking, but we were hoping she would meet us afterward and bring a few of her friends, like Cinderella.

She never did.

California's Disneyland was in Anaheim, just a few miles from The Plush. Getting an early start (if you consider noon and early start), we spent the entire day there. To be frank, it was a little disappointing in the magic department. Although it had the rides and attractions we found so magical at Disney World in Orlando, it just wasn't the same. The park itself was located only a couple hundred yards from the main road, so you could see the Magic Castle as you drove by.

Walt Disney took such care in providing you with a magical journey into Disney World, this seemed almost an afterthought. Of course, Disneyland is practically 20 years older than Disney World, so it seemed they took the time to make improvements to the "experience" in Florida.

There was no mystery as you parked your car and walked to the main entrance. It was like going to the mall. You could still hear the traffic on Harbor Blvd and Interstate 5 while inside the park. It was a little disappointing as far as the atmosphere, but the rest of the park was A+ all the way.

It was still crowded, but nothing like we encountered at Disney World. However, the characters portraying "Alice in Wonderland" and "Cinderella" were just as cute and, unfortunately, for us, just as mute.

We struck out once again with the costumed characters, but we were determined to give it another shot the next day since we had 2-day tickets.

"I think we need a different approach," the Catman plotted. "Maybe I'll write her a note and slip it to her so she doesn't get in trouble?"

The Catman is always working it.

One thing about Disneyland, they didn't serve alcohol. What

we didn't realize at the time was how close the parking area was to the entrances and exits. When you leave, they stamp your hand for a free return at any time. Had we known that, we would have packed the cooler and stepped out of the park periodically for the pause that refreshes. I made a mental note to bring the cooler when we came back tomorrow.

# the NBC Studio Tour

We were star-struck while sitting in the front row, dead center of the stage, less than 50 feet from Johnny Carson's desk.

There, right in front of us, was a small white star painted on the dark blue studio floor. In show business, it's called a "mark." Carson would stand on that star as he delivered every monologue on *The Tonight Show*. If you closed your eyes, you could hear the horn section lead the rest of the band blasting the show's opening theme music at a high decibel level as the studio audience breaks into sustained applause. Ed McMahon, standing slightly offstage to the left, grabs a microphone and opens the show with, "Frroooooooomm Hollywood, it's *The Tonight Show Starring Johnny Carson!*" before launching into the names of tonight's guests. As the band dramatically fades out and the audience quiets, the drummer begins laying down a long drum roll, accompanying Ed as he takes his time delivering the phrase everyone came to hear, "And now, ladies and gentlemen, Heeeeeeeeeerrre's Johnny!"

With that, the band and the audience explode into a frenzy. From backstage, someone opens a slit in the middle of the giant, multi-colored curtain, and out strolls Johnny Carson. The always perfectly dressed Carson walks into the spotlight and is smiling and laughing, acknowledging the band and Ed as he makes his way to the center of the stage floor, drawn to that white star, like a moth to a flame. Staring out into the audience and making eye contact with everyone, Carson soaks up the applause. Hands in his pockets, he bows to the crowd, waiting for the uproar to die down so he can begin delivering his monologue.

But Johnny wasn't standing on his mark in the middle of the stage floor.

The band wasn't playing the theme song, and there was no sign of Ed McMahon.

Although we were really sitting in the half-darkened studio where they shoot *The Tonight Show*, it was as part of the tour group, not the audience during a live show. The NBC Studio Tour included a visit to the iconic "Studio 1" and saved it for last.

We spent the previous 90 minutes or so as part of a 20-person group, led by a pretty NBC tour guide named Jenny, through the bowels and intricacies of the Burbank Studios. For me, a television junkie, this was worth every penny of the $2.50 ticket price.

Since arriving in LA on Monday and all the horrors associated with our first day here, we visited Universal Studios on Tuesday, then spent all day Wednesday at Disneyland in Anaheim. Thanks to the advice from Richie at "Tickets Galore!," today we were positioning ourselves to get free tickets to see Carson tomorrow night.

We booked a room at The Baja Motel, across the street from the NBC Studios, and would spend most of Thursday night into Friday waiting on the ticket line, where they distributed the complimentary tickets the next morning.

Our plan was foolproof...

On Thursday morning, we packed our bags and checked out of the Plush Horse Inn. I expertly canceled our last two days to the chagrin of the desk clerk, who seemed disappointed we weren't staying with them anymore. Heading straight to The Baja Motel, we arrived at about 10:30, but our room wouldn't be ready until about 3 pm. They took our bags for safekeeping and gave us a parking permit so we wouldn't get towed.

It wasn't rated five-stars, but what motel is? They had a pool with chairs and brightly colored umbrellas. We hoofed it across the street toward the NBC lobby entrance on West Alameda Avenue. There we encountered about 60 people gathering under a long awning attached to the building, leading into the main lobby entrance.

Thinking this might be the line for the studio tour, I asked someone.

"No way, man," the guy said, "We're waiting to see the Carson show."

The Carson show?

It was only 11 am. What were they doing waiting in line eight hours before the show tapes?

"Don't you already have tickets?" I asked innocently, assuming if you secured tickets, you just arrived at 5:30 for the taping.

"Yeah, we got tickets," someone else said, displaying their ducats and slurring their speech like they had been drinking all morning, "But you still gotta freakin' wait in line. The tickets don't automatically get you inside, man. It sucks, but it's worth it. This is my third time, man. Carson is the King!"

This was a little disconcerting, but we didn't have time to get all the details. Our tour was to start in a few minutes.

We walked past the ticket holders and made our way into the main lobby of the building, which anchored the corner of West Alameda and West Olive. The entrance was surrounded on both sides by floor to ceiling windows. The high ceiling held black and white glass chandeliers, giving it a modern look. There was a bit of an echo in the cavernous lobby area.

A blonde receptionist sat behind a half-circle desk with a large, colorful NBC Peacock logo on the wall behind her. She wore a half headset, with a black sponge-like headphone covering her right ear. There was a microphone protruding from the headset that wrapped around to the front of her ruby red lips. The modern-looking desk had a computer and a bank of phone buttons with little square lights blinking.

"Good morning and welcome to NBC," she chirped, greeting us before the doors behind us even closed. "Are you guys here for the 11 am tour?"

Before we even had a chance to acknowledge, she pointed to our left and said, "The group is assembling right down there."

Without saying a word, we marched like good soldiers to join the group. She then morphed into receptionist mode, seemingly talking to herself as she pressed one of those blinking buttons. "Thank you for calling NBC, how may I direct your call?"

Such efficiency.

Just outside the lobby area, near the elevators, we could see people through a set of glass doors. To get to them, you needed the security guy to buzz you through. Two older gentlemen were sitting to the right of the doors behind a corner kiosk that contained numerous black-and-white security video screens displaying a variety of areas around the complex.

We waved our tickets at them, causing one of them to reach for a buzzer under the desk that automatically opened the doors for us, and we passed through.

That's where we met up with our tour guide, the beautiful Jenny. She was corralling about 15 people standing near the elevators for the 11 am tour.

"Hello!" she greeted us as the doors closed behind us with a loud clang. "You guys here for the tour?"

We joined the group milling about as she collected our tickets.

She had the brightest, bluest eyes I had ever seen. She was built specifically for this job.

"I'm getting a chubby," the Catman whispered to Mr. B as he stared at her behind and took a picture of it.

"You get a chubby when the wind blows," Mr. B answered.

Jenny showed us a bunch of cool things during the tour, including stops at the wardrobe department and the KNBC News studio. We ventured out into the staff parking lot and saw Johnny Carson's parking spot (it was empty) and the famous NBC Commissary (which we weren't allowed to eat in).

The last stop on the NBC Tour was what we came for, Studio 1, where they taped *The Tonight Show with Johnny Carson*.

After taking the elevator to the second floor, the doors opened into a vast, industrial-looking corridor. Although the tile floors were just as clean and shiny as those in the lobby, the 25-foot high ceiling was lined with dual rows of fluorescent lights, looking more like the hallway leading to an insane asylum than an iconic TV show. If it weren't for the giant sign touting "*The Tonight Show with Johnny Carson*," painted on the white cinderblock walls, you would think you were in a warehouse.

When entering the studio, your first thought was it looks way too small. On television, you get the impression of a sizable sprawling studio with a thousand audience members. In reality, there seemed to be no more than 300 seats, arranged in three sections, a left, middle and right, tapering down from long rows at the top to shorter rows in the front. Other than it being very tall, it was not unlike a large movie theatre.

The dark blue cushioned seats resembled those in a high school auditorium. We entered the studio through the center concourse on the stage floor, and sat in the first two rows.

It was almost surreal to be sitting just 40 feet from Carson's iconic desk, where he interviewed movie stars and celebrities seated on the couch. The center of the studio was backed by the 20-foot-high blue, yellow, and pink curtain. The highly polished stage floor is a dark blue, matching the seats, with a single white star painted in the middle, Carson's "mark" when delivering his monologue. Although it was not visible when you watched on TV, you could clearly see it from the audience. The seats for the band were on the right side of the stage.

Jenny explained the history of the show, told us the view of Los Angeles that is behind Carson's desk is made of cardboard and showed us the "Applause" signs. She spent about 10 minutes answering questions about guests on the show and the show's stars, Carson, Ed McMahon, and Doc Severinsen. Surprisingly, nobody asked how they could get tickets to the show.

So, I did.

"The tickets are free to the public," she said, "But they are very limited."

"How limited?" I followed up.

"They only distribute between 50 and 75 tickets to the public for each show," she clarified, "But even if you get a ticket, you may not get into the studio."

She explained that the studio only holds 250 people and most of the tickets are distributed to special guests, sponsors, and VIP's. "Depending on that night's guests," she continued, "they may have less than 50 seats left, so even if you have a ticket, there may not be room in the studio."

"Well, that's a drag," I said, getting a chuckle from the rest of our group.

"They start to distribute the tickets at 8 am," she said, "But most of the people on the line have been there since about 2 or 3 in the morning. An NBC Page will begin issuing numbered cards about 6 am to the first 100 people waiting in line."

"I thought you said only 50 to 75 tickets were available to be given out?" Mr. B jumped in with.

"Again, it depends on the guests for that show," she said. "The show's producers deliver the complimentary tickets to the box office just a few minutes before it opens at 8 am."

"What about all those people we saw waiting outside with tick-ets?" the Catman asked, "Aren't they getting into the studio tonight to see the show?"

"Maybe," she said with a smile, "They don't start loading the public until all the invited guests have been seated in the studio. The people waiting in line are used to fill the remaining seats."

Well, that wasn't going to happen to us.

As we left the studio and headed back to The Baja for some R&R, I asked a guy positioned near the front of the line, what time he arrived at the box office last night.

"About 2 am," he said.

Good to know.

We still had the second day of tickets for Disneyland to use later that afternoon. The plan was to visit Disney until it closed, and head back to The Baja for a quick nap before securing a spot on the line.

What could possibly go wrong?

The Baja Motel didn't have a 5-star rating, but it was just what we were looking for at the time. The place was only about 300 yards from the NBC ticket office and even had a pool, something they didn't have at The Plush Horse Inn.

The complex was "L" shaped with about 20 units on two floors. The upper rooms had balconies overlooking the parking lot. The redwood railings contrasted nicely with the yellow stucco walls, and the balusters alternated between redwood and black. Instead of a single entrance door, each room came with sliding glass doors.

After completing the NBC Studio Tour, we spent most of the afternoon in the pool at the far end of the parking lot. There were plenty of lounge chairs available inside the chain-link enclosure. We grabbed a small table that was adorned with a red, white, and yellow umbrella, to hold our trusty Styrofoam cooler filled with Coors.

It was the middle of the afternoon, and the place was mostly empty. We had the pool to ourselves for about an hour, until people started returning from their day trips. Unfortunately for us bachelors, the pool area began filling with families and little kids with floaties. That was our cue to head back to the room.

Before leaving for Anaheim and our second day with Mickey Mouse, we stopped at a deli and got sandwiches and more beer. We packed the cooler, then hung out in the parking lot like we were tailgating at a ball game. By the time we got into the park around 7 pm, we were feeling pretty good.

While walking around the park late in the evening, we stopped to listen to the "Poppa Do-Run-Run" band that was performing a set of rock-n-roll songs. To our surprise, they broke into a medley of songs that included a few bars of Springsteen's "Born to Run." Bruce reached into his pocket and pulled out a joint. "You know what that means," he said with a gleam in his eye.

"Are you fucking nuts?" I asked him. "How are we supposed to pull this off?" To be honest, I didn't even know he brought a joint with him.

"It's dark now," he said, "There are plenty of bushes and hiding places over by the bathrooms."

"Great," I said sarcastically, "I guess since no one could see us, they won't be able to smell it either."

"Exactly," he said.

Well, a pact is a pact…

With the Catman as a lookout, we found a secluded spot behind the bathrooms and sat down behind some bushes to smoke. The rest of the evening went pretty well if I do say so myself.

Since it was our last night in Disneyland, we stayed for the impressive firework show over the Magic Castle before heading back to the car. Even though the park was still open for another hour, we were done and ready to head out. So was most everyone else.

The lines to get out of the parking lot were ridiculous, so we decided to stay in the car and finish the last few beers we had in the cooler. By the time the lines to get out began moving again, we were out of beer. What timing!

It was a straight run from Disneyland to Burbank on Interstate 5, but about half-way into the 40-mile trip, I wished I had peed before we left.

# the Ticket Fiasco

It was a little after midnight when we got back to Burbank after spending the evening at Disneyland.

"Let's turn down the block by the ticket office," the Catman suggested from the backseat. He wanted to see if the ticket line for *The Tonight Show* had started forming yet.

I told him it was a complete waste of time. The NBC tour guide said the line starts forming about 2 am. Besides, I had to pee like a racehorse. We sat in the Disney parking lot for a long time once we left the park. Apparently, everyone else decided to exit at the same time. Driving to the NBC ticket office would require following a one-way road past The Baja and around the park at the end of the block. To get back to The Baja, you had to circumvent the entire studio complex.

"My back teeth are floating," I told him as I pulled off the main road and headed to the parking lot of The Baja. "Besides, it's faster if you just walk down the block."

I barely made it into the bathroom before I had to let go. Oh, what a relief! Mr. B followed right behind me, but he had to pinch a loaf, so he might be in there for a while.

After setting the alarm for 2 am, I crashed on the bed and began mindlessly flipping through the TV channels. Just then, Catman burst into the room, almost out of breath.

"There's a lot of people on the line already," he blurted out while grabbing a pillow and one of the extra blankets from the closet. "We better get out there right now, or we're never getting tickets!"

"You're shitting me," I said. "That's impossible."

"Impossible or not," the Catman countered, "There's a lot of fucking people on that line, and it's only 12:15. Someone told me Farrah Fawcett is the guest tomorrow. Farrah-Fucking-Fawcett! I'm going right now."

There wasn't a teenage boy in America that didn't have a Farrah Fawcett "nipple" poster on their wall.

But there was no way I was heading out of this room. I was so freaking comfortable.

"Save me a spot," I said, turning the TV off and burying my head into the pillow. "I'll see you in two hours."

And with that, the Catman grabbed a beer from the cooler and headed out the door.

When Mr. B emerged from the bathroom, I updated him on the current situation. He decided to join the Catman out on the line but was going to light up a bowl before leaving. I was asleep before he even had the bowl packed.

I almost didn't react when the alarm clock began ringing at 2 am.

I swept my hand across the night table and knocked over two empty beer cans before locating the alarm clock. Without looking, I pressed every button I could, but nothing stopped the incessant beeping. I flipped over on my side, found the cord, and yanked it from the wall.

Mission accomplished.

Pulling on a pair of shorts and grabbing my pillow and blanket, I trudged out of my comfy room to meet the boys. I found them sitting with their backs against the building wall and chatting with the people behind them on the line.

"Well, look what the cat dragged in," Mr. B laughed as I strolled up to them, "Maybe you should go to the back of the line, buddy."

"Go fuck yourself," I said as I wedged my weary ass between the two of them and sat down.

"I should have just taken a power nap," I lamented, "I slept too long. Now I feel like shit."

The couple behind us in line introduced themselves as George and Kathy from Virginia Beach. When they found out Bruce and Sal called me "Disco," George stood up and did the John Travolta pose from *Saturday Night Fever*. I explained that the nickname was not related to the music. He seemed disappointed. We chatted for about an hour before Mr. B and the Catman headed back to the room to pee. It was after 3 am by the time they got back.

While they were gone, I stood up and did a preliminary count of the people in front of us and came up with about 45. Based on what the NBC tour guide had told us, they only give out about 50 tickets if there is a famous celebrity guest. Who's more popular than Farrah Fawcett? This might actually work out.

I guess I fell asleep before they even got back.

I woke up about 5:30 am and stood up to stretch my aching body. Many of the people on the line were now stirring and doing the same thing. The sun wouldn't be rising for about an hour, and it was still very dark out. Mr. B and Sal were dead asleep along with Kathy and George.

Squatting up and down like a marathon runner limbering up before a race, I reached down to pick up my pillow and blanket and bring it back to the room. Mr. B reached out and grabbed my arm.

"Where are you going?" he mumbled.

"I'm gonna bring this stuff back to the room, pee, and brush my teeth," I whispered.

"No, you're not," he insisted. "They're handing out numbers in a few minutes, and you have to be here on the line."

He was right, of course. Only people on the line would get numbers, no excuses.

"But, I have to pee."

He pointed to a row of bushes across the street and said, "Use that as a bathroom. If you go back to the room, you might sit on the bed and fall asleep, you dickwad."

He was right about that, too.

I decided to hold it in until I got my number.

At precisely 6 am, someone wearing the familiar NBC blue blazer opened the door by the ticket office and walked out into the street to address the crowd.

"Good morning, everyone!" he said cheerfully as the crowd applauded, "My name is Charlie, and I work for NBC. I'm going to begin distributing these numbered ticket squares." He was holding a stack of cardboard squares in one hand and waving one of them in the air with the other.

He explained that the first 100 people on the line would be given a number, and when the ticket office opened at 8 am, they would begin distributing the complimentary tickets for tonight's show. Only people with numbers get a ticket. Once all the tickets for that night's show are gone, that was that.

"Before I give out the numbers," he said, "I want to make sure you all understand how this process works."

Charlie informed everyone they tape the show at 5:30, so they don't begin filling the studio with the people holding the free tickets until about 5 pm. That's going to require a day-long commitment of ticket holders waiting outside the studio from 8 am until 5 pm.

"The tickets are complimentary," he warned us, "But they do not guarantee admittance to the show."

It was quite a shock to George and Kathy, but we heard the same thing yesterday during the tour.

After taking a few questions and making sure everyone felt comfortable with the process, Charlie began distributing the numbered cards. In my head, I was mentally counting each card he handed out as he moved closer to us.

It was going to be close.

The Catman got #50, Mr. B got #51, and I got #52. If they only gave out 50 tickets, we were screwed. So were George and Kathy. They got #53 and #54.

"You better pray they give out more than 50 tickets today," I told the Catman, "Otherwise, you're not going."

"That's bullshit, I'm going," he insisted, "I'm not missing a chance to see Farrah."

"And what the hell are we supposed to do while you're in the studio getting a hard-on?" Mr. B asked.

"Not my problem," Catman replied, "Besides, maybe we'll all get tickets, right? We don't know how many tickets are being given out."

"How about this?" I said, trying to come up with a contingency plan, "If we all don't get tickets, we'll just pack up and go to San Diego today. We'll come back here Sunday night and try for tickets to Monday's show? Our flight to Phoenix isn't until nine at night, we'll have plenty of time to see the show taping at 5:30. Whadda ya say?"

"Works for me," Mr. B chimed in.

"Of course, it works for you," Catman replied. "You're #51."

I still had to pee, so I pocketed my trusty #52 card, and duck-walked back to the room. Mr. B was right, once again. I just wanted to lay my head down on the bed for one minute. I knew what a mistake that would be, so I went back and joined my compadres.

The ticket office opened at precisely 8 am and began distributing the tickets. We noticed that some people, as soon as they got their tickets, took off like jackrabbits, racing to the ticket holder's waiting area by the main lobby, passing others who were casually walking.

When the Catman approached the window, he collected a ticket and began to do a happy dance. When Bruce presented his #51 card, the woman behind the glass politely told him they were out of tickets.

Fuck.

"Oh, come on!" Mr. B lamented.

I poked my head into her view and said, "Please, the three of us are together. Can't you spare two more tickets?"

"I'm sorry," she said, holding up two empty hands. "They only gave me 50 tickets. I don't have any more to give out, even if I wanted to, I'm sorry."

Mr. B then looked at the Catman, who was no longer performing the happy dance. "Looks like you got a great souvenir, Catman," he said.

A defeated Catman pocketed his souvenir ticket, and we headed back to The Baja. There was no need to stay here anymore, so we canceled our last night and packed our stuff. Instead, we would head to San Diego today and spend the weekend with my uncle.

# SAN DIEGO

# San Diego

Snakes...

Ocean Beach

Uncle Mickey

Shaving Beers

The "King"

A Two-Fer

Catman Frizbee

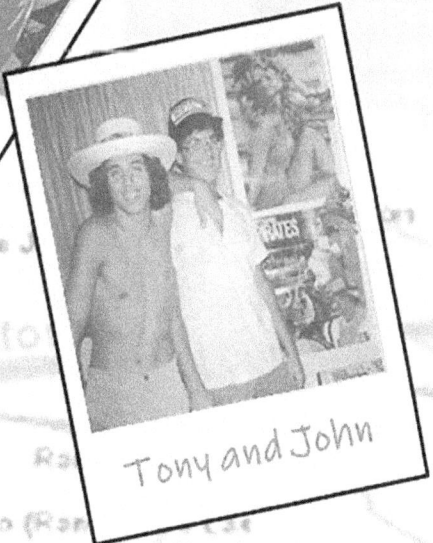

Tony and John

# It's Gone

Our Uncle Mickey had initially moved from Brooklyn to New Mexico back in 1971 before settling in El Cajon, San Diego a few years later. Sal and I hadn't seen him, my Aunt Lillian, or my cousins Tony and John since then. He was a delivery driver for Wonder Bread in Southern California. Family means everything to Italians, and there was no way we could visit the West Coast without seeing them.

We were a little dejected over the ticket fiasco as we packed our stuff, but also looking forward to San Diego. The Catman was more bummed than us since he had a golden ticket he was never going to use.

"Listen, Catman," I said, stuffing my dirty clothes into a garbage bag. We were hoping to do laundry when we got to San Diego. "I wanted to see Carson even more than you. You're more bummed because you're missing Farrah."

"And your point is?" Catman asked.

"Yeah, Disco," Mr. B chimed in, "I'm bummed we didn't get to see the Queen of the Nipple."

"We saw the Carson studio, right?" I offered in my own defense, "Even if she was wearing a wet T-Shirt, we couldn't see that famous nipple from where our seats would be. The show is the experience, not the guest. We want to be part of the live audience and experience the band, the monologue, the bad jokes. What difference does the guest make?

"Farrah Fawcett-Fucking-Majors, you dipshit," Catman replied. "Maybe if you didn't have to pee, we would have driven down the street, saw the line forming, and I would have jumped out to get on the line. We wasted almost 15 minutes. All we needed was to be in front of two people, and we all get tickets."

He was right, of course.

"Tell you what," I offered, "Let's come back to The Baja on Sunday. We'll get on the line before midnight; that way, we will be assured of getting tickets for Monday's show. The show tapes at 5:30 in the afternoon, we'll have plenty of time to make our flight, too. It's not until nine o'clock. Whaddya say?"

"Fuck The Baja," Mr. B countered, "Let's just go straight to the line and sleep out."

"Works for me," the Catman agreed, "But I want to go straight to the beach when we get to San Diego. I want to see blondes in bikinis."

We settled up with the clerk at The Baja and loaded the cooler with the remaining beers. Wearing our bathing suits, we took a couple of towels from the bathroom and snatched one of the bedspreads to use on the beach. If that makes us criminals, well, maybe the statute of limitations has been reached?

I stuffed my ever-growing brochure collection into the glove compartment. We put two suitcases and the cooler into the trunk along with one of the laundry bags. The other suitcase went into the back seat, along with the two other laundry bags. Unfortunately for the Catman, he usually sat in the back and would be stuck with the stink. We drove most of the way with windows cracked open.

It took about two hours on the I-5 southbound, which runs right along the coast, to get to San Diego. Before heading East towards El Cajon, we took the Catman's suggestion and drove down near the beaches. Since he didn't get to see Farrah because of me, I was pretty much going to be his bitch for the rest of the day. We decided to stop at Ocean Beach, which was about 20 minutes from El Cajon.

The parking lot was not crowded, but Mr. B picked out a spot for us in an area near some bushes.

"Let's head over there so we could smoke a bowl before we go down to the water," he said.

It sounded like a good idea to me. We found a spot between two deserted cars and set up shop.

Although we couldn't see the beach or the water through the dense bushes, you could hear the constant sound of the waves crashing in the distance. The privacy bushes were protecting a grassy area that was reserved for picnic tables, and we could hear snippets of conversations wafting through the shrubbery.

We closed the windows, cranked up the A/C and kept the car running so we could stay cool and listen to the radio. There was no one in sight as Mr. B packed the bowl, lit the flame, and started the party.

We still had plenty of pot left over, even though we had smoked a shit-ton of it every day. What were we going to do with the leftovers before getting on the plane tomorrow?

"What if you put it inside your sock?" Mr. B posed to me.

"Are you insane?" I shot back. "I'm not putting it in my sock. You put it in your fucking sock."

The Catman chimed in, "What if we bought something like a

box of candy, stuffed it in there, and put it inside the checked luggage?"

"Don't they screen the luggage?" I asked innocently.

"Maybe we should just concentrate on smoking the rest of it?" suggested Mr. B. Although it was a noble thought, that just wasn't happening without us ending up in a hospital. "Either way, when we get to Arizona, Felix and Kozshekka will have plenty."

He was right, they would have plenty.

"I'll roll a couple of joints to take with us on the beach," Bruce said. As was his usual MO, he gave two of them to me and kept two for himself. We always put them into our wallets so they would retain their shape, but just flatten out a little.

We shared not one but two bowls between the three of us, and there was a great cloud building up in the car. We cracked the windows so the smoke could escape slowly instead of the nuclear bomb mushroom effect. There was nothing like the smell of a car full of reefer smoke and dirty laundry.

Bruce stuffed the remaining pot and all the accoutrements back into the glove compartment and we staggered out of the car to grab some beers out of the cooler. "Let's do some recon before we bring all the stuff down," the Catman offered. We quaffed the beers and headed onto the beach through the main entrance, a large curved archway.

The vast expanse of the beach took me by surprise. It was a long way from the boardwalk to the water. I use the term boardwalk loosely because it wasn't made of boards, as you see in New York. It was made of cement.

The concrete plaza stretched along a row of businesses; bars, food stands, and beach shops stretched for a few hundred yards. It was separated from the sand by a three-foot-high brick barrier wall that had access openings every hundred feet or so. Dotted along the barrier were sturdy white light posts, about 8-feet high. The plaza widened as you got closer to the restaurants to accommodate outdoor tables and chairs.

The surf-shop rented all types of beach-going equipment, like umbrellas, colorful beach chairs, and boogie boards. There were plenty of surfers way out in the deeper water, catching the bigger waves. Although it was a Friday morning in the middle of August, the beach was not as crowded as I expected. I guess when you have weather like this every day, it's not necessary to take advantage of it like you would in New York.

In the middle of the plaza was a large tower-like structure painted blue that was taller than the other buildings. The top-level reached about two floors above the stores. It was lined with large windows around the front three sides, giving it a clear view of the beach. It looked like an air traffic controller tower at a small airport. On the roof was a long, bending flagpole with an American flag being pulled in the same direction as the breeze.

There was a wide opening in the barrier wall directly in front of the tower. The area on the sand was roped off by two lines of bright red ropes, lining a 20-foot path from the tower directly to the water, which was more than a football field away.

"What the fuck is that?" the Catman asked.

"I think it's where the lifeguards hang out," answered Bruce, pointing to the surf. "Look at the edge of the water. There are no lifeguard stands."

He was right.

We had never been to a beach where there were no wooden lifeguard stands. In New York, lifeguards were stationed every 100 feet or so and just a few feet from the waterline. The lifeguards perched at the top of the stands, wearing sunglasses, hats, and white stuff on their noses, surveying the water in front of them. Attached to the side of the white structures were all the lifesaving tools they needed – floats, rope, and boards. Draped around their necks were whistles to use as a warning when someone got too deep.

But there was none of that on this San Diego beach. Although all beachgoers respected that rescue lane between the two red ropes, I was concerned a 100-yard sprint along the sand could cost someone their life. Running on sand is extremely hard to do if you want to get somewhere quickly.

The plaza was filled with some of the most beautiful people, both men and women, but especially women, that we had ever seen. Quite frankly, it was almost embarrassing for us to even be allowed on this beach. We had lost whatever tan we had built up before the trip running around like tourists. Although we weren't pasty white, we certainly weren't sporting the same bronze beauty look everyone else was. Besides, none of us were blonde.

"I think I'm getting a chub," the Catman said with a smile. I think we were all getting a chub, but I wasn't about to check everyone's package.

"Let's go get our shit and grab some rays," Mr. B said, leading us back to the car.

I was smiling like a kid in an ice cream parlor as I opened the trunk to get the cooler out. I noticed Catman was peering into the passenger window.

"Mr. B, did you leave the glove compartment open?" he asked.

Sure enough, all the brochures I had been collecting were scattered on the floor in front of the passenger seat with the compartment door opened awkwardly, facing straight down.

"What the fuck?" Mr. B said.

I put the key in the lock to open the door and get a closer look, but it wasn't necessary. The door was already unlocked. Upon further review, both doors were unlocked.

Someone had broken into the car.

"Oh shit," I said. "Grab my suitcase. I have all the plane tickets there." My suitcase was in the back seat, but it was still zipped shut.

Mr. B was sifting through the brochures on the floor and

fiddling with the compartment door, which was not cooperating. I opened the zipped compartment on my suitcase, and found the tickets safely inside, thank goodness. I heard Mr. B say something but couldn't quite make it out at first.

Then he repeated it.

"It's gone," he said. "The hooch. It's fucking gone. So are the pipe and the rolling papers. They even took the goddamned lighter."

Sons of bitches.

We were only gone for about 15 minutes. Someone must have seen us smoking in the car and took advantage of the opportunity to boost our hooch. We searched around the parking lot to see if we could find anyone smoking in their car, but apparently, no one else was as stupid as we were.

"The Lord giveth," Bruce said philosophically. "And The Lord taketh away."

He was right, of course.

We were lucky to have anything at all on this trip, and to have it stolen at the end of the California portion of our journey was almost poetic.

There was not much we could do about the theft. What were we going to do, call the cops? Nothing else was missing. It was just a huge bummer.

I pulled out my wallet and opened it, exposing the two joints Mr. B had rolled before. "I guess we'll have to ration these over the next 48 hours."

"Exactly," Mr. Bruce agreed. Then he opened his wallet and took one of his joints out and put it in his mouth. "Anyone got a light?"

The Catman, who always carried a lighter in case some chick needed a light, said, "I have a torch." We shared the joint and cursed our carelessness.

Mr. B grabbed the cooler from the trunk, and I grabbed the

bedspread and the towels. We were still going to have a good time on the beach, no matter what. We headed back to the main entrance and out onto the concrete plaza.

As Bruce and I made our way down to the beach, the Catman decided to hang around the plaza and do some serious girl watching. Not that there weren't plenty of girls to watch on the beach, but the Catman always liked to get up close and personal when he could. He floated over to the "Shake Shack" to get his MAC on.

The beach sand was much whiter than in New York, where it's more tinged with grey. Unlike New York, the water was filled with surfers taking advantage of the bigger waves further away from the shore.

We set the bedspread and cooler onto a spot between some blankets, cracked open a cold one, and walked down to the water. Looking out into the Pacific Ocean, we stood with huge smiles on our faces.

"Is this the best, or what?" Mr. B asked.

The waves were cresting their white foam in contrast to the blue water. As the water made its way over our feet and past us, it returned to the ocean dragging sand and eroding us about a half-inch under the surface. When the wave returned, it deposited sand on top of our feet, and when it drew back out, it removed another half-inch from under them. Before we knew it, all we could see was our ankles.

"This is just like Jones Beach," I deadpanned, "Except there's no trash on the sand, the water is crystal clear, and there isn't a fat person in sight." We looked around and found plenty of trash cans embedded in the sand for people to get rid of their garbage. "Why don't they do that for us in New York?"

"Because people in New York are fucking slobs," Mr. B answered. "You think they're going to walk five feet to put their shit in a trashcan?"

Of course, he was right.

Just then, a loud siren emanated from the tower above the plaza, followed by the crackle of a microphone and a message that was repeated twice, "Attention, attention. Please stay clear of the rescue zone."

We turned around to see four lifeguards, wearing black surfing wetsuits with bright red trim, tearing across the concrete plaza with small yellow floats in their hands. They flew across the sand, barely making impressions. Within just a few seconds, they were launching themselves over the waves and into the ocean.

So much for being slowed down by the sand.

We joined the gathering crowd along the sides of the rescue zone as more lifeguards from the tower came running down with emergency equipment to the edge of the water. Everyone was holding their breath and straining to find the lifeguards who went into the water.

As they emerged from the deep waters, they were carrying a kid who must have been surfing, as he was in a full wet suit also. The EMT's, now on the edge of the water, took over, attending to the surfer immediately on the wet sand. With more than 50 people watching silently, they tried to revive the kid. When he sat up to spit water out of his mouth, we all broke into cheers. The lifeguards and EMTs strolled back up to their tower through the empty rescue zone like ball players heading to the locker room after winning the game. They waived to the cheering throng like heroes, which indeed they were.

After seeing that, we didn't really feel like going too deep into the water, so we just went in and out to get some saltwater on our bodies to help us cook in the sun. We returned to our bedspread, rolled the towels into pillows, and took our positions to get some rays. I closed my eyes for a few minutes, but the sun was so hot, I decided to reach into the cooler and get another beer. I spied the chicks on the blanket next to us and noticed they were facing the wrong direction. Instead of their feet facing the water, their feet were pointing at the plaza.

I opened the beer and sprinkled some ice water on Mr. B, who was relaxing peacefully.

"Take a look at this,'" I said to him, pointing to the trio next to us. "Do you notice anything unusual?"

"You mean besides their bush bumps?" Mr. B said with a smile.

"Not that, you pervert," I said, although they did have great bush bumps, "Look at which direction they're facing."

This got his attention, and he sat up.

"Why are they facing that way?" he asked.

Now sitting up, he looked around. Some were laying on blankets, others in small beach chairs, but all were facing the same direction. We were the only nimrods facing the water. Just then, the Catman came over.

"This place is fucking nuts, boys," he said with a huge smile. "I met so many cool chicks so far. I got two numbers! We can go to a party tonight if we want."

"How old are these chicks," I asked.

"I don't know," Catman replied, "I didn't ask. Maybe High School seniors?"

"Or maybe jailbait," said Mr. B, "Don't you know 16 will get you 20?"

"By the way," the Catman inquired, "Why are you guys facing the wrong direction? Don't you know the sun rises in the East and sets in the West?

We looked at him quizzically.

"So, who gives a shit?" Mr. B retorted. "Does it go in the other direction on the West coast?"

"No, you dickwad," Catman laughed, "But on the East Coast, the water is on the other side, so in the morning, the sun is rising over the water. On the West Coast, it sets over the water, so everyone out here faces east in the morning to get the sun."

"And you know that because...?" Mr. B asked.

"Unlike you jackoffs," Catman said, "I'm actually trying to get laid, so I need to talk to chicks. I was hanging out with Beverley and her friends, and I told them I was here with you guys. I saw you down on the beach and pointed in your direction. I said we're from New York. That's when they started to laugh."

"Laugh?" I questioned. "Why were they laughing?"

"First, I thought they were making fun of my accent," he said, "But then they pointed to you guys and said you were facing the wrong way like all people from the East Coast."

"Fuck them," Bruce said. "I don't give a shit. I'll do whatever the hell I want, man." And he laid back down, feet to the water.

"He's right," I echoed. "I can't face the wrong way either. It just doesn't feel right."

I joined Mr. B in his silent protest.

"You guys are assholes," said Catman as he turned to face the way the rest of the West Coast faces, head to the ocean. "I think I might have a shot with Beverly." He closed his eyes and drifted off into never-never land.

That's when Mr. Bruce waved to the girls to get their attention, picked up the cooler, and poured some of the melting ice water over Catman's head. He screamed like a little girl. They howled with laughter and headed back into the Shake Shack.

We hung out on the beach for a little, then decided to get some lunch before heading out to El Cajon for dinner with my uncle later. Acting like good San Diegans, we threw all our empties into the trash cans, then emptied the remaining cooler water onto the sand. Like the New Yorkers we really were, we left the motel bedspread and the rolled-up towels on the beach.

It was almost one o'clock now, and we saw some of the natives turning around to follow the path of the sun and get maximum exposure. Soon, it looked like a New York beach with everyone facing the relentless waves.

We stopped into the Shake Shack for a burger and a few beers, hoping to see Beverley and her friends, but they were long gone. We headed back to the car, suddenly realizing again that we were "weedless."

Well, we still had three bullets left in the gun and a few more days left in California…

At just 21 years old, I hadn't been to a lot of other places.

Maybe it was my fear of flying, but like most of my friends, I needed to work to pay for school. That didn't leave a lot of money for other activities except partying. You don't get a lot of paid vacation days when you work part-time at the mall.

Don't get me wrong, we went on plenty of road trips (within reason), but unless our parents were footing the bill, we weren't heading to Europe any time soon. Other than that road trip down to Florida in 1977, my world had been limited to the Northeast. No matter where you go in the Northeast, the weather is basically the same.

August in Los Angeles was a lot like August in New York, hot and sticky. But San Diego was something completely different. The weather was, in a word, perfect. It wasn't humid, although it was in the '80s the weekend we spent in El Cajon. The days were pleasant, and the evenings were cool and breezy.

"It's like this every Goddamn day," my Uncle Mickey told us. "You can't beat this weather! All the dirt, grime, taxes, and bullshit in New York—they can have it. I don't miss it one goddamn bit."

My Uncle Mickey was the first-born male of seven children, including my mother and my Aunt Jean, Sal's mother. He was also the biggest personality of them all. At 39, he was a large, gregarious man who swore like the U.S. Marine he was. After almost 10 years away from Brooklyn, his New York accent was beginning to fade. However, his thick, dark hair and pear-shaped physique made him stick out like a sore thumb in the land of bronzed beauties and blondes. To me, he was a sight for sore eyes.

His go-to outfit for the weekend was an Italian-style, sleeveless white T-shirt with shorts and sandals. He always seemed to have a spatula in his hand, either cooking breakfast or tending the BBQ.

Uncle Mickey and Aunt Lillian lived in a ranch style house on Sheila Street in the San Diego suburb of El Cajon, not far from the Air and Space Museum. They escaped New York back in 1971 for New Mexico before resettling to San Diego in 1975. Other than an occasional visit back to New York, our family hadn't seen them very often. We hadn't seen our cousins Tony and John in six or seven years. Tony was now 17, and John was close to 13.

After a most triumphant first couple of days in Los Angeles, including finding a bag of weed in the bathroom of the Los Angeles airport, our luck had unfortunately turned. We spent overnight waiting in line for tickets to see Johnny Carson, only to be denied when they ran out after the Catman got his. Today, someone stole the miracle bag of weed Bruce found in a bathroom stall at the LAX Airport from our car in the Ocean Beach parking lot.

Licking our wounds, we pulled into the Motel 6 in El Cajon to secure lodging for the next couple of days. We were just a few miles from Uncle Mickey and would be having dinner with them tonight. The place was nothing to write home about, but it wasn't going to break the bank.

"It's not so bad," I offered, as we pulled into the parking lot. "It looks like there's a fresh coat of paint on the outside."

"This place looks like my ass on a rainy day," Mr. B said. He always did have a way with words.

There weren't a lot of local options, and we didn't feel like traveling back toward the Interstate. It was only for two nights, so we decided to stay.

"Welcome to Motel 6," the clerk behind the counter said, greeting us as he emerged from the back room, wiping his hands on a small dishrag. The little bell over the front door alerted him to our presence when we walked into the lobby. "How can I help you today?"

He was in his mid-thirties and starting to lose his hair. There was a dingy white t-shirt underneath his open vest. If he had a hat on his head, I would have sworn he was Ed Norton from *The Honeymooners*. It was quite a contrast to the beautiful people we encountered behind registration desks all week.

"You guys looking for a couple of rooms?" he inquired, reaching under the counter and producing a sizeable leather-covered register. He paged through it until finding a half-filled page, then turned it to face me.

"No thanks, one room will be fine," I answered, grabbing one of the pens from the small cup, scribbling our names under the column marked "Guest" and then "Massapequa, New York" under the heading for "City and State."

"All right," he said, turning the book around so he could review what I had written, "Just so you know, the rooms have only two queen beds in them."

That's when Mr. B grabbed the Catman by the shoulders and kissed him on the cheek. "No worries," he said, "We're homosexuals."

"Don't look at me," I said, as the shocked clerk glanced in my direction. "I just take the pictures."

I grabbed a few more brochures for local attractions to add to my collection, grabbed the keys (there were only two guest keys for each room), and we headed to room 118. It was on the lower floor of the two-story structure, about as far away from the front desk as possible. There were no cars in front of doors 114 through 117, so maybe the clerk was sending us a message?

The last time we showered was at The Baja on Thursday morning, and I'm sure we still had the stink of sleeping on concrete combined with a few hours at the beach. There were only three towels on the rack, but at least we had soap and shampoo in the shower.

"Call that dude at the front desk and get some more towels," I instructed Catman, as I grabbed one off the rack outside the bathroom. "We're going to need more tomorrow anyway."

"Don't forget to ask him for some lube," Mr. B added with a laugh, as he fiddled with the clock radio.

I closed the bathroom door and waited for the water in the shower to heat up. I have a thing about building up steam in the bathroom for when I'm finished showering. Bruce must have found a rock station, as I could hear the muffled ending to a Beach Boys song. The shower was surprisingly strong and hot. With the water pounding on my head, I was almost in a trance when someone opened the bathroom door.

As the amassing steam quickly escaped, I could clearly hear Springsteen's "Candy's Room" playing on the radio. Sure enough, it was Mr. B keeping up with the Springsteen Burn and holding a lit joint over the top of the shower curtain.

A deal is a deal.

While Mr. B was taking his shower, the Catman was relaxing on the bed and perusing some of the San Diego brochures I collected from the lobby. I wasn't really paying him any attention while getting dressed, except he was cracking his knuckles very loudly. Like close cousins, we have spent our entire lives together, and he always seemed to be able to crack his knuckles, even as kids, almost on cue.

"How can you do that all the time?" I asked.

"Do what?" he responded.

"How can you crack your knuckles like that?" I said. "I can crack my knuckles, but not all the time. Once I crack them, I can't crack them again a second time."

"It's a talent," he laughed. "Sometimes I don't even know I'm doing it. I can do it on all my fingers and toes."

Toes?

"Get the fuck outta here," I said, waving my hands at him in disbelief.

Just then, Mr. B came into the room, wrapped in a towel.

"What's going on, boys?" he said with a smile.

"The Catman claims he can crack every knuckle on both his fingers and toes on command," I said, bringing him up to speed.

"Get the fuck outta here," Mr. B repeated.

"Watch and learn," The Catman said confidently.

With military precision, the Catman began with all the fingers on his right hand, then moving effortlessly to those on his left hand. Each one echoed a sharp, loud crack. It was disgusting, yet beautiful.

We saved our applause for the end when by just bending each individual toe, he snapped off a surprisingly loud crack. It was magnificent, yet repulsive.

"Encore, encore!" Mr. B sarcastically demanded.

"OK," said the Catman, wanting to oblige.

What could he possibly do for an encore?

The Catman sat on the edge of the bed and stuck his legs straight out. He then proceeded to crack his ankles, earning a standing ovation.

It's the little things in life that you really appreciate.

---

Italian families are naturally close. My mother and father had six brothers and sisters each. My life growing up was filled with aunts, uncles, and cousins, almost 24 hours a day. I didn't have a lot of friends as a kid, not because I couldn't make friends, I just didn't need them.

There were celebrations scheduled almost every weekend. Birthdays, holidays, Communions, and Sundays were mandatory reasons to get together. Italians would congregate just to celebrate a child's moving up a shoe size if they had to.

After Uncle Mickey and Aunt Lillian left New York for good, we never lost touch with them. But, we certainly didn't see them often with 3,000 miles between us. Sal and I were not going to pass up an opportunity to see them while out West. Bruce, who has been as much a part of my family as any friend I've ever had, was also looking forward to meeting Uncle Mickey for the first time. He knew all my other aunts and uncles from family gatherings at my mother's house. To us, he was the fifth Beatle.

Growing up, my cousins Tony and John were as much a part of

our get-togethers as anyone. In Italian families, it doesn't matter how long you are apart. Once you see each other, you pick up right where you left off. It's like slipping back into a comfortable pair of jeans. It just feels great to wear them again.

When we pulled into their driveway, my now 17-year old cousin Tony was the first to greet us.

"Oh my God!" he exclaimed, "I can't believe you guys are here!"

He rushed to bearhug Sal, as he was the first to get out of the car. Right behind Tony was my Uncle Mickey, looking tanned and more relaxed than I ever remember seeing him.

We hugged long and hard without really saying anything. Suddenly we were transported back to the safety and security of Grandma's basement. Family really is everything.

"So, who's this," he said, pointing to Bruce.

Mr. B stuck his hand out to shake, but instead, Uncle Mickey gave him a bear hug just like he did with Sal and me. That's how we Italians roll.

Aunt Lilly was in the kitchen, preparing a salad for dinner when we came inside. She was so happy to see us, I thought I detected a little tear in her eyes.

Uncle Mickey, who was tending to the BBQ, joined us in the kitchen carrying some beers.

"Now that you guys are old enough," he said, "I guess you bastards can join your uncle in a few beers, right?" We were happy to oblige him.

While in the middle of enjoying burgers and hot dogs, my other cousin John came home from baseball practice to join in the festivities. He was just a baby the last time I saw him.

We spent most of the evening catching up on family updates and reminiscing. That's how we found out my cousin Tony is a snake lover. As kids, he always had the wildest stories for us. We were a little older and knew he was just making things up, but we still went along with him because it was fun, and he had such a great imagination.

He was telling a whopper about the snakes he had in his room and how each one of them had their own, individually locked cage for everyone's protection.

Did he say cage?

"If they got out," he told us, "They could kill you."

Thinking back to the 10-year-old version of my cousin Tony, I politely smiled and was about to call "Bullshit" on my now 17-year-old cousin. He must have sensed my disbelief.

"Ya wanna see them?" he teased.

Immediately, my Aunt Lillian forbade him. "Anthony," she said sternly, using his given name, "You are NOT taking those things out of their cages. Do you understand?"

Things?

But it was way too late. He was already half-way down the hallway and ignoring her completely.

Looking over at my Uncle Mickey, I saw he had a big smile on his face. "Wait till you see what he's got in there."

When he summoned us from inside his room, I didn't know what to expect. I thought he might have a snake or two inside a little cage or fish tank. To make things more dramatic, when we followed him to his room, the door was closed.

"Just a second," he said from behind the door. After a short pause, he announced, "Come on in," and Sal opened the door.

I couldn't believe what I saw.

He was standing in the middle of the room shirtless, with a six or seven-foot-long, red-tail boa constrictor wrapped around his neck. On top of his head was a white Panama hat that had a smaller, Columbian red-tailed boa, wrapped around it. Inside his room, he had three cages, one still occupied by a huge Burmese Python. The cages were three and four feet tall.

I was the last one to enter the room, and the first one to exit.

"He's not kidding," My Uncle Mickey commented, "If that thing gets out of the cage, it could kill you."

Suddenly, our room at the Motel 6 was looking more like the Taj Mahal to me.

On Saturday, with Uncle Mickey working, we spent the day at Ocean Beach, returning to the scene of the crime we could never tell them about. When we got back, we played some wiffle ball with John, fully expecting to mangle and embarrass the poor child with our athletic prowess. Instead, we barely touched his fastball. Not quite 13 years old, he made us look like ridiculous old men, flailing away as he struck us out with ease.

That night, at the Catman's insistence, we tagged along with Tony and some of his friends for a typical teenager night, playing some mini-golf and hanging out at an ice cream place. The girls (and guys) were one more beautiful than the other. Everyone was tanned and mostly blonde.

This was going to be our last night in San Diego as we would be heading back to Los Angeles Sunday night to get one last shot at tickets for Monday's Johnny Carson show.

---

We never actually unpacked our bags when we arrived at the Motel 6 on Friday, so there wasn't much to do that morning before checking out. Uncle Mickey had insisted we come for Sunday morning breakfast before leaving. I found Mr. B perusing some of the tourist brochures sitting on the table while I was stuffing the last of my dirty laundry into a plastic trash bag.

"Maybe we should see downtown San Diego today?" he suggested, looking at the brochures for the aquarium and the zoo.

"Sounds good to me," I said, noting that I'd like to get some laundry done when we get to my Uncle's house. "My shit's really starting to stink."

"Starting?" the Catman said, chiming in.

Mr. B grabbed the brochure for the NBC Studio Tour, and we discussed logistics for later in the evening.

"Wasn't there a park near that hotel we stayed at," Mr. B asked?

Catman, our Navigation Specialist, pulled out our trusty map, located the Burbank studios, and sure enough, there was a little park around the corner.

"We can park there, catch a few zzz's and then get on the line at 2 am," Mr. B suggested.

"No way," said the Catman. "I'm not taking any chances. I'll go straight to the line when we get there to get us a spot."

I grabbed one of the blankets from the closet to use when we got to Burbank and threw it into the car.

Uncle Mickey was already working the stove with his trusty spatula when we arrived. Once again, his sleeveless Italian t-shirt was his wardrobe choice for the day.

"We got eggs, bacon, and sausage," he said with his trademark smile. "What'll it be, boys?"

"What, no steak?" Mr. B commented, with a big grin on his face.

"I'll give you steak, you bastard," Uncle Mickey shot back with a laugh, pointing the spatula at Bruce like it was a sword. We told him about our nightmare first night in LA and how we took advantage of our free breakfast. He just smiled.

"Good to hear that you guys didn't give in!" he said proudly. "Those sons of bitches always try to take advantage of people. I miss that about New York. Out here, everyone is so passive, we New Yorkers sometimes stick out like a sore thumb."

"Do they try to take advantage of you, too?" Sal asked.

"Oh sure," he replied. "They try to take advantage of everyone. But I don't let those bastards get away with anything. They see me coming, they don't even try anymore."

Then he laughed long and loud. We laughed right along with him.

Aunt Lilly grabbed our laundry bags and offered to take care of our laundry while we were out with Tony and John for the afternoon. We told them of our plan to sleep out in Burbank for a chance to get tickets to see Johnny Carson.

Although my Aunt Lilly thought it was a terrible idea, I could see a devilish smile on my Uncle Mickey's face.

"We were so close last time," I said. "We may never get this chance again."

We enjoyed the day with our cousins as they took us into downtown San Diego. When we got back, we had a great dinner of barbecued chicken and ribs, packed our luggage with clean laundry (Thanks, Aunt Lillian!), and were ready to head out.

"You guys better be careful," my uncle quietly whispered as we were getting ready to leave. "There are strange and dangerous people everywhere."

Like every Italian family does when it's time to say goodbye, we hugged for a long time. I hadn't seen him much since he left the East Coast about 10 years before, other than when he made the occasional trip back home.

Little did I know I would never see him again. He died in 1986.

# BURBANK

# Burbank

Line Beers

The King

The Goddamn
405 (again)

Chillin' At
The Baja

The MAC Daddy

Car Beers

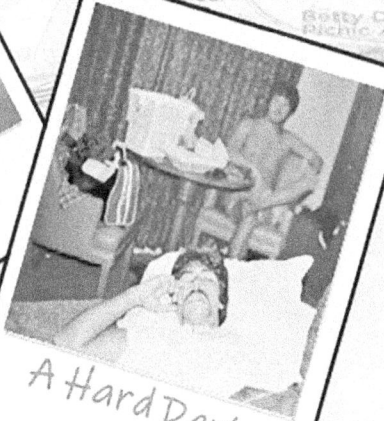

A Hard Day's
Night

# the Second Chance

We headed north on the San Diego Freeway (I-5) sometime after 9 pm. The trip to LA took a little over two hours, and by the time we got to Burbank, it was approaching midnight. We dropped the Catman off by the ticket window for the studio. There were only about 20 people in front of him on the line.

"Let's hope this works," Mr. B said, as the Catman got out of the car.

"Don't leave me hanging, you guys," Catman replied. "They

start handing out the numbers around 6 am. If I get a ticket, this time, I'm going."

We learned our lesson the hard way. On Friday, they issued about 75 numbers (our numbers were 50, 51, and 52), but that show had a big name guest, Farrah Fawcett-Majors. When they started distributing the complimentary tickets at 8 am, they only had 50 tickets to give away. Sal held ticket #50. Bruce and I were shit out of luck.

The guests booked for the Monday show, however, were not exactly "A-Listers," so we had a better chance of getting tickets. Either way, we weren't going to take any chances.

"We'll be back in an hour or two and hang out with you," I promised.

He grabbed the blanket and went to the end of the line, giving us the thumbs up. Before we even pulled away, a group of four were behind him in the queue. They also had blankets and pillows. I guess they had done this before.

We drove the Chevy around the corner and located the entrance to the park. Finding a secluded place, we settled comfortably into our seats to grab a few zzz's. I set my watch alarm for 2 am so Catman didn't have to spend the entire night alone on the line.

The radio DJ was spinning some good tunes when we heard the haunting strings and piano intro to Springsteen's "Jungleland" drifting out of the speakers. Looking at Bruce, he was already reaching for the lighter while I grabbed one of the remaining doobies out of my wallet. We had successfully accomplished our "Springsteen Burn" pledge every time we heard a Springsteen song since we got out here. There was no reason to break that streak now. We decided to smoke just half of it and save some for tomorrow.

It was now after midnight, and the DJ announced he had an advanced copy of the new "Who" album, *Who Are You?* and was about to play it in its entirety. Without any words being passed, Mr.

B lit up the other half of that joint. At the same time, we enjoyed the album debut with the rest of Southern California.

The alarm knocked me out of a sound sleep. I'm not sure I heard the last few songs of the album, but it was time to keep our promise and join the Catman. I roused the sleeping Mr. B, and we headed out. It wasn't a far walk, but as we approached the line, it was much longer than when we left the Catman two hours ago.

We found him talking to one of the chicks ahead of him in the line (of course) and took our places next to him.

"You guys look like shit," he commented.

Without a mirror to confirm, we just took his word for it. There were several additional people in front of us now, as more lazy bastards like us joined their friends who were also keeping a place in line. Soon, all of us were in la-la-land as we snoozed while waiting for the number guy to show up at 6 am.

Right on cue, around 6 am, the NBC Page wearing the blue blazer adorned with the iconic multi-colored peacock emerged from the ticket office. He had a stack of little cardboard squares that had numbers written on them. This time, we were given number cards 38, 39, and 40, which put us in an excellent position to score tickets for the show.

Having done this before, we already knew the drill. Although there were public restrooms available in the park, Bruce and I opted for the bushes across the street. When we got back, the Catman took care of his business. That started a steady stream of people, mostly men, crossing the street and returning with a relieved look on their faces.

At precisely 8 am, that same NBC Page emerged and welcomed everyone again, thanking us for our patience. Once again, he went through the ticket distribution process speech we heard on Friday.

After explaining how obtaining complimentary tickets did not necessarily guarantee you entry into the studio, someone from the back of the line yelled, "That sounds like bullshit." Everyone laughed.

This time, we didn't care. We learned from the NBC Studio tour about waiting with the other ticket holders. If necessary, we would run over people to get a better spot on ticket holders' line up the block.

The distribution line moved orderly, and we finally got our golden tickets. After a quick high-five, we tore ass down the long block, passing a few people along the way who were taking their time. When we got to the corner, there were only about 30 people in front of us. It was 8:23 am, and we still had about eight hours to wait, but by God, this time, we were getting in!

———

You learn the fine art of "socialization" after spending a few hours isolated on a line with your immediate neighbors. With everyone in the same predicament, you begin to develop a kinship, a sort of "bunker" mentality. I've spent a lot of time waiting in line for tickets to concerts or playoff games. Bonding with people in your immediate vicinity is easy because no one strays too far away from the line.

While sharing a sense of excitement, there is a mutual understanding of the plight we are faced with. Without a guarantee of getting into the show, we collectively wait for several hours until a final determination is made. Most will get in, some will not.

Within the framework of sharing this common situation, there are unwritten rules of "Line Etiquette" to be followed:

- Once the line is established, members of your immediate group can leave for a few minutes to get supplies or take a bio-break. They can't return with any additional people. That will not be tolerated. You can bet the people immediately behind you know exactly how many are in your group.

- It's always good form when leaving to get provisions, to offer your take-out service to the people immediately before and after you. You've been bonding for a few hours, swapping stories, and sharing limited supplies. It's the proper thing to do. When stepping out for a soda or a snack, be polite, and ask your neighbors if they need anything, within reason. Unfortunately, the group 10 spots behind you is shit out of luck. You have to draw the line somewhere.

- Don't offer to pay upfront for anyone's food or drink order and expect to settle when you get back. There's always a chance when you get back, they only have large bills, and you are not "The Good Humor Man" sporting a change-making belt. Nothing wrecks the fragile vibe between line sitters than a tiff over money. You're still trapped with these people for a few more hours. Take cash upfront, and if the change is reasonable, keep it for the effort, don't even offer it back. You earned it since you jack-assed across the street for them.

- Keep the conversation light and comfortable. Small talk is the best option. Stay away from political and religious topics. It's fun to talk to people from different parts of the country, but they are strangers. You never know what might set someone off.

- If you are from New York, you are right, and everyone else is wrong. That's just how it is. Tourists seem to give you a different level of respect when they find out. A New York reputation, deserved or not, is a welcome addition to your arsenal in the world of small talk. When you speak, people listen. They better listen.

The main entrance to the NBC Burbank Studios was the corner of West Alameda Avenue, where it intersects triangularly with West Olive Avenue. Both avenues have two lanes of traffic and turning lanes. With the Burbank Studio housing hundreds of employees, the food choices from the local stores were plentiful. There were restaurants, a taco place, a deli, and a pizza place.

The giant glass doors of the lobby entrance faced West Alameda. Running down West Olive were office windows with an extended canopy, offering relief from the hot sun. The line started about 50 feet from the main entrance, so as not to impede foot traffic, and snaked its way down the side of the building on West Olive, under the canopy.

The canopy provided the much-needed shade that made sitting on the concrete bearable. The wide sidewalk allowed us to lean against the side of the building comfortably, legs stretched out. Several entrepreneurs made a few bucks hawking ice cream, candy bars, and soft drinks (no beer) to the line sitters.

As soon as we were settled, I noticed some people had little coolers with them. Since nobody was breaking their balls about having a cooler, I volunteered to retrieve ours. We still had a few beers in it, but the ice was gone. This cooler had seen better days, but it only cost us a buck and lasted the entire week. We wouldn't have any use for it after today since we were headed straight to the airport after the show.

Returning with the cooler to our spot in line, I was hailed as a conquering hero by our non-cooler friends directly behind us. Immediately, Roger offered to make a deli run for some rolls, coffee, and a six-pack of beer if he could put some beer in our cooler.

"Tell you what," I offered, "You get the breakfast; I'll get the ice and some more beer." A kinship was born, and together, we carefully negotiated the traffic to cross West Olive. The deli had a well-stocked refrigerated section with soda and beer. There was also a self-serve soda fountain with different sized cups. Roger picked out a six of Budweiser and poured two sodas with ice from the fountain, before ordering rolls with butter for all of us. I picked up two sixes of Coors and a bag of ice.

When we returned, Mr. B came running over to meet us at the curb. "Keep the beer in the bag," he said. "One of the NBC people just came out to tell us you can't have any open alcoholic containers on the line. We're out on the sidewalk, man. He said the cops would issue tickets."

Bummer.

Well, a simple thing like that wasn't going to stop us. "I got an idea," I said, handing Bruce the bag. Sprinting across the street to the deli, I grabbed a few soda cups, covers, and straws from the fountain area. I held the cup upside down while passing the counter guy to show him they were empty, and he gave me a "thumbs up."

Problem solved.

An NBC Page had gone over the ground rules while I was across the street. She recommended using the payphone to call the pizza place across the street, whose number was displayed larger than life in the window. They opened around lunchtime and delivered heroes and pizza to people in the line. Since the main lobby was now open, there were restrooms available if we needed them. She also reminded everyone to always leave at least one member of the group on the line. Cigarette smoking was allowed, but please, no cigars.

"She was a doll," Catman noted about the NBC Page. "I have to get her name next time she comes out. Who knows, right?"

"You realize the last time you showered was the day before yesterday," I reminded him, "And you just spent the night sleeping on the concrete outside the box office. Not to mention, your breath must fucking stink right now."

He leaned over to me, opened his mouth, and puffed air out directly in my face. "Get the fuck away from me, you..." and I had to stop. His breath didn't stink at all. Actually, it smelled like spearmint.

I cupped my hand over my mouth and blew into it. It reeked like a camel's asshole. "How does your breath not reek?"

The little bastard was chewing gum.

"I always have gum on me," Catman said while smiling. "You never know when you are going to have a close encounter with a good-looking chick, right? I'm always prepared."

The Catman is always working.

Around lunchtime, Roger asked if we wanted to split a pizza with him and his girl, but we politely declined. The last time we tried California pizza, it really sucked. Instead, Catman ventured out to the deli and got a few sandwiches. We were quietly eating our sandwiches and sipping beer through a straw when I dropped my half-empty cup, spilling it on my sneakers.

"Son of a bitch," I said, reacting instinctively.

The older couple a few people down from us seemed a little upset as the guy turned and said, "Can you guys watch what you're doing?" He had been keeping tabs on us most of the morning, although we weren't paying any attention to him.

His wife grabbed his arm and said, "Honey, leave them alone. They didn't get any on us." Then he gave me the "stink-eye" and went back to his business as I refilled my cup with a fresh beer.

Just then, his wife lit up a cigarette.

"Be careful honey," he said sarcastically, "If you get that flame too close to them, they might explode," laughing as he said it.

I smiled and gave him a little chuckle as I held up a fresh beer cup, saluted him with it, and took a swig from the straw.

That's when Mr. B leaned over and yelled, "BOOM!"

Around 2 pm, things were getting tired and dull, so Bruce and I slipped out and went back to the car to smoke the remaining joint and listen to the radio for a few minutes. As the joint burned down to the last inch, there was about one hit left for each of us.

"I can't believe this is the last of it," I lamented to Bruce, carefully handing him the rapidly reducing joint. "What were the chances of you finding a bag of hooch in the crapper?"

Mr. B inhaled his last toke and held it for a few extra seconds before blowing the smoke out of his nose. "I'd say the odds were astronomical," he said, handing me the rapidly shrinking roach for one more hit. "But just wait until we get to Arizona. That's going to be a foggy couple of days with Felix and Kozshekka."

Following Mr. B's lead, I also savored my last hit, slowly letting the smoke escape through my nostrils.

When we got back to reality, things were starting to heat up.

It seemed we were not the only people on the line drinking out of soda cups. A group of older people behind us had been drinking wine all day and were starting to feel their oats. The pretty NBC Page came out about 3 pm to see how everyone was doing. Noticing her ID tag said, "Becky," I told the Catman her name, and he gave me the thumbs up.

"We're doing great, Honey!" someone from the group of inpatient wine drinkers shouted. "When the hell are you going to start letting us in? This is getting ridiculous!"

"Sir," Becky responded, "We don't actually begin filling the studio until about 4:30 or 5 pm, but we appreciate your patience." Before leaving, she gave us a bright and cheery, "Thank you, everyone!" and went back inside.

Just then, a much larger NBC Page emerged who looked more like the Incredible Hulk, except he wasn't green or wearing purple shorts. He resembled William 'The Refrigerator' Perry, who played football for the Chicago Bears in 1985. 'The Fridge' was a massive defensive lineman who ate quarterbacks for breakfast. The studio-issued navy-blue NBC blazer was at least one size too small for his frame. His rectangular name tag with the colorful NBC peacock logo, which simply said "Darnell," was dwarfed by the breastbone it was attached to. With his bright white button-down shirt stretched across his torso, his contrasting blue tie was too perfectly tied not to be a clip-on, but who would have the nerve to ask?

He slowly made his way down the line, making eye-contact with everyone as he approached the wine-drinking lightweights who were being rowdy. We couldn't hear what he was saying, but they calmed down very quickly, responding with a few "Yes, sirs" and "No, sirs."

Striding back to the main entrance without saying a word, the massive Darnell followed Becky back inside. It had been a long day, but we were ready. We were pumped.

There was only one question remaining.

Was Johnny Carson ready for us?

# the Tonight Show

Even with tickets, we still weren't assured of getting inside the studio. After spending eight hours on a line outside the studio entrance, drinking and eating, and drinking some more, there was no guarantee.

The perky NBC Page who had been keeping us informed,

popped out from behind the glass doors about 4:30 with another update.

"Hello again, everyone," she smiled, displaying a mouthful of beautiful white teeth, "We're going to start loading the studio in about 15 minutes. Please make sure you have all your personal items with you when we start moving. I know it's been a long day, and we just want you to know how much we appreciate your patience and cooperation. Thanks again and see you all inside!"

A loud roar came from the line of ticket holders. We had been instrumental in making sure most of our linemates were not only well-fed, but well-juiced, just like us. Although I'm sure that deli catered to *Tonight Show* ticket holders for many years, I'll bet this was the first time that deli sold their entire stock of cold beer. Last time I looked, they were also running out of soda cups.

The disclaimer on the back of the complimentary orange ticket reminded us, "Ticket distribution is in excess of studio capacity. Guests will be seated on a first-come, first-serve business. Admission is not guaranteed." Of course, we still needed to behave because "NBC Reserves the right to revoke this ticket at any time."

And we had behaved ourselves, to a certain extent. We dedicated a lot of time and effort to see a live *Tonight Show* taping, so we weren't going to blow it before getting inside the door. With only about 30 or so people in front of us, there was an excellent chance we would get inside.

We chugged the last of our beers without using the straws. We dragged the Styrofoam cooler filled with empty beer bottles next to one of the already overflowing garbage containers lining the curb. This was the last time we were going to see that cooler; it had served us well.

This was it; we were going inside!

"Let's make a pact," Mr. B suggested. "If anyone mentions 'New York,' we go crazy, OK?"

"Define crazy," the Catman requested.

"You know," Mr. B offered, "jump up and down and yell like crazy!"

It sounded good to me.

"What if no one mentions New York during the show?" I asked innocently.

"Then we yell and holler when they mention any place at all," he calmly replied. "Who's going to know? Besides, I didn't wait in line all fucking day to sit in my chair and politely applaud. We're New Yorkers. It's our job to be rowdy!"

Again, Mr. B hit the nail on the head.

When pretty Becky came out for the last time, around 4:45, to cheers and applause, the Incredible Hulk was right behind her. As we approached Becky at the lobby door, dutifully handing her our tickets, the Hulk was eyeing each of us as we entered, making sure that we knew he was large, and still in charge.

There was no doubt in my mind who was in charge.

The sudden giddiness of the people in line didn't wholly dissipate as we followed Becky in an orderly fashion into the air-conditioned lobby. Many of us, who just a few minutes ago were whooping and hollering, quieted down for some final instructions. The floors were perfectly buffed as you could see the reflection of the ceiling lights in the geometric patterns of the tile. The overall feel of the room was more like the quiet reflection and murmuring of a museum lobby.

"Thank you all again for being so patient," Becky's voice echoed inside the cavernous lobby. There were still many disappointed people way in the back of the line who just didn't get in this time. After admitting the first 40 people (which thankfully included us), she told those remaining in the line that once everyone inside was seated, she would return for the rest of them if seating permits.

"Welcome to *The Tonight Show!* You made it! Give yourselves a round of applause!!" she said as we awoke from our spell and began cheering and applauding. "We're going to bring you up to Studio 1, where the show is taped, using the elevators on your right."

The walls of the lobby area around the elevators were adorned with posters of many iconic NBC shows. The Hulk in the NBC blazer stayed in the lobby with us as Becky filled the car, returning in a few minutes to reload. We made it during the third trip and were led from the second-floor lobby into the main studio entrance.

When entering the studio through the center concourse, we were just a few feet from the stage. The seats in the front rows we occupied during the studio tour a few days ago were already filled. Actually, most of the audience was already seated and quietly chatting. Only the last two rows at the top of the studio were partially empty.

Another NBC Page directed us to the top rows of seats on the left side of the studio, looking down at the stage. Johnny would be looking to his right to see us. We learned during the studio tour about the design of the audience seats back in the '50s by Jack Paar, the original host of *The Tonight Show*. The rows were graduated steeply so that the audience members in the higher rows would be closer to the stage. We were guided to three seats at the end of the aisle, just one row from the top. Catman moved in with Bruce sitting next to him. I sat in the end seat. We had a good look at Johnny's couch, which was right below us.

The last two rows were for the non-VIPs and uninvited guests, basically, the 50 or so schmucks who spent six hours sleeping on concrete, then waiting eight hours to get in. There was still a full row, maybe 30 or more seats behind us that could be filled. That was good news for the people behind us on the line. I was imagining how happy they were going to be when Becky returned and let them in the building. It looked to me like everyone was getting a seat this time.

Three behemoth cameras roved the floor like droids from the *Star Wars* movies, controlled by cameramen wearing headsets. The famous band was on the right side of the stage (to Johnny's left) just past the giant, 20-foot high, multi-colored curtain that centers the studio.

There were six television screens mounted on the ceilings which displayed the live TV feed, like you would see in your living room. From our vantage point, we had a full view of the high-gloss blue stage floor with the tiny white star painted in the middle. That's where Carson would stand when delivering his monologue in a few minutes.

"This is unbelievable," the Catman offered as we settled into our seats. We were still feeling the effects of an all-day burn, but at that moment, we were like little kids in a toy store for the first time.

"This is sooo cool," I added, "I can't believe we're actually here."

"Don't forget," Mr. B said, "If they mention New York, we're gonna bring this house down!"

We all nodded in agreement.

Bruce spied a head of beautifully flowing blonde hair a few rows in front of us. "Hey Catman," he kidded, pointing to the woman, "Maybe that's Farrah! Want me to see if I can get her autograph?"

"Go fuck yourself," Catman replied.

*Tonight Show* producer Freddie De Cordova came out a few minutes before anyone else to welcome us and lay down some ground rules. He pointed out and explained the various "Applause" signs around the studio, hanging from the ceiling like the TV monitors. There was no smoking during the show taping and, if we had to use the restrooms, now would be a good time. They would only allow you to leave the studio if there was an emergency. During the commercial breaks, if we wanted to stand up, stretch our legs, or dance to the music, feel free to do so.

The crowd cheered when he told us Carson would be hosting tonight but informed us Ed McMahon was on vacation. Doc Severinsen would serve as Johnny's co-host, while Tommie Newsome conducted the band.

Just then, *The Tonight Show*'s band began to take their seats, followed by Newsome, who waved to the crowd. After warming up, the group launched into a couple of songs to entertain us for a few minutes. They sounded great! Newsome then grabbed a microphone to introduce Severinsen. He popped out from the side of the stage wearing a long-tailed, dark navy-blue, Admiral Duhey jacket with bright white trim around the lapels and pockets. Underneath was an open-collared white shirt with blue stripes. The top three buttons of the shirt were undone, draping the collar over the top of the jacket lapels.

Severinsen made some jokes about Ed McMahon being out on a bender and unavailable. After talking about the guests, he invited us to, "Get ready to have a good time!" We whooped and hollered with the rest of the audience.

We were ready, we were pumped!

The God-damned, motherfucking *Tonight Show*!

As Doc walked off the stage floor to the podium just below our section on the left side, the studio lights darkened, and the stage lights came on. You could hear De Cordova counting out the last few seconds, "5, 4, 3, 2, 1" as the band broke into the iconic theme music. On cue, Severinsen took a deep breath before elongating the first word, just as you hear every night in your living room.

"Froooommmm Hollywood, it's *The Tonight Show Starring Johnny Carson*!"

We all joined in when the applause sign started blinking. We were on our way!

"Johnny's guests tonight are Ardath Evitt, actress Bess Armstrong, author Elia Kazan, and comedian Bobby Kelton," Severinsen read from the oversized index cards he was holding. Then he paused as the band quieted to just a drumroll, and launched into, "And now, ladies and gentlemen, Heeeeeeeeerrrreeee's Johnny!"

At that moment, a small opening appeared through the giant

center stage curtain, and Carson walked out. We stood and applauded with most of the people in the upper rows, as he positioned himself over the white star on the blue stage floor.

He was sporting a light blue or gray checkered suit, perfectly tailored, with a matching light blue shirt and a wide, '70s style tie. The large knot was perched at the top of his collar, which obediently stayed down without the benefit of oxford buttons. The necktie itself contained broad, dark navy stripes, highlighted by thin black and white stripes, and was neatly tucked inside the buttoned suit jacket.

After a few minutes of soaking in the adulation, he held his hands out, instructing the crowd to calm down so he could begin the monologue. It was a little surreal seeing Johnny Carson as a small figure standing on a stage in front of us, while simultaneously seeing him larger than life on the TV monitors.

Delivering his monologue with the usual mixture of groan-inducing jokes, we laughed out loud along with him when he knew he had produced a bomb. There was no distracting chatter in the audience as he continued telling jokes and trying hard to entertain us.

After one particularly bad joke, he said, "Let's change the subject, shall we?" and we all laughed with some people applauding approvingly. "Not sure if you know this," he continued, "but there is still a newspaper strike in New York."

Hearing the magic words, the three of us jumped up out of our seats and started whooping and hollering, just like we promised. Unfortunately, we were the only one's whooping and hollering.

The usually unflappable Carson seemed stunned at first, stopping dead in his tracks and looking up to where we were standing and yelling. As the audience howled, he looked back at the camera, pointed in our direction and deadpanned, "Obviously some non-readers from New York," causing the audience to erupt with laughter.

The Master burned us on National television!

With the audience still laughing, we continued to whoop and holler. I turned to high-five the Catman and Mr. B when I spied the hulking Darnell making his way up the aisle toward us like he was chasing a quarterback. Without saying a word, he was pointing at us and signaling us to sit down, which we obliged as Carson continued with the rest of his monologue.

Darnell stood like a prison guard over my left shoulder for the remainder of the monologue. I could almost feel his breath on my neck as he silently waited for the commercial break. When Johnny performed his trademark golf swing leading into the commercial break, the band began playing music.

Once the cameras were off and the staff began buzzing around on the studio floor, Darnell put his large meat hook of a hand on my left shoulder.  Leaning in and pointing to all three of us, he whispered, "If you do that again, I am going to throw all your asses out of here, understood?"

I proactively put my hand on Bruce's shoulder to prevent him from rising and confronting this mass of human muscle to my immediate left. I looked Darnell in the eye and replied, "Yes, sir. No problem."

He looked at Bruce with the stink eye and said, "I'm not kidding. Have a good time and enjoy yourselves, just don't interrupt the show again or all of you are history."

We settled down as Darnell walked up the last two rows and took a folded arms position, standing right behind our section.

Bruce mumbled, "That's bullshit, man. He can't tell us what to do. I'll fucking yell if I want to yell. What kind of shit is that?"

I turned to him and said, "We have to be cool, man, and just not interrupt."

"I don't care," he continued, "if anyone mentions New York again, I'm standing up and yelling. I don't give a fuck what 'Gigantor' says."

Although I didn't doubt him for a minute, I wasn't looking forward to being dragged out by my heels. Thank goodness nobody mentioned New York for the rest of the show.

While coming out of the commercial break, the audience applauded as the band was finishing up a song. Just as the cameras came back to show a closeup of Johnny now sitting at the desk, someone off-camera threw a pencil to him. He just reached up and caught it, almost without looking, then twirled it through his fingers as a high school majorette would do with a baton. The audience howled and cheered, causing him to once again acknowledge the rowdiness of the crowd.

He looked at Doc and said, "Man, they must be passing something around in the audience tonight! Either that or it must be the full moon." We howled and cheered with the rest of the audience as Bruce stood up to wave at Darnell, who just shook his head, smiled, and waved back.

Before bringing on the first guest, Ardath Evitt, who parachuted on her 74th birthday for the first time, Johnny did a bit about specialty magazines, showing some of their favorites. He pointed out that a magazine named *"Popular Nazi"* touted about "Learning the Goosestep" and another, *"The National Lighthouse Keeper,"* ran a story about "50 Ways to Excite an Aircraft Carrier with Finger Shadows." He ended with *"Wine-O Quarterly"* and their featured stories, "How to Make Wine in Your Shoe" and "A Confirmed Alcoholic Tells How He Used His Liver to Get His Car Started." That had the audience howling and applauding. Johnny said, "Somehow, I had a feeling this was the crowd for that joke! We'll be right back…"

The rest of the show was almost forgettable, although the 74-year-old parachutist was a hoot. Bess Armstrong talked about her new movie, "How to Pick up Girls," which the Catman commented was probably his life story. Comedian Bobby Kelton did a funny few minutes. The show ended with author Elia Kazan talking about his new book, "Acts of Love." There was no musical guest.

When the show was over, we exited through the doors at the top of the studio, passing our pal Darnell. He smiled at us as we walked past and said, "Thanks for cooperating, guys." Mr. B then reached out to shake his hand. When Darnell offered his in return, I thought for sure Mr. B was going to pull back and wisecrack something. I didn't see the need for us to look like black-eyed raccoons by the time the evening was over. Instead, he pulled out his best "Eddie Haskell" impression and said, "No hard feelings, Big Guy, right?" and winked at Darnell. The Big Guy winked back, and all was well with the world.

The show finished taping about 6:30, and we had to catch a flight at 9 pm. We beat it out of there and headed south on the 405 to LAX. It was about a 30-mile ride, but all we saw in front of us was taillights.

We were back in the teeth of the Los Angeles rush hour on a Monday Night...

# the Rental Car Rematch

By now, we were masters of the Los Angeles freeways. Unfortunately, there was no escaping the Los Angeles traffic. We made our way to the 405, which would take us right into LAX.

Before leaving the park, we spent about 15 minutes cleaning all the junk out of the car to make it look presentable before returning it. Besides the beer cans and assorted debris, we found matchbook covers and even more brochures for tourist attractions. How many did we actually have in that glove compartment?

By the time we negotiated the early evening traffic on the 405, it was almost 7:30. Our flight was at 9 o'clock, but we still had to return the rental car. We pulled into the drop-off lot and were immediately greeted by an attendant. He was wearing the standard Dollar-Rent-A-Car uniform with a red collared golf shirt adorned with a name tag that said, "Jake." He was carrying a clipboard with a retractable point pen, attached with a small string so he wouldn't lose it.

A quick inspection of the car was required before settling the bill at the front desk, and Jake was just the guy to do it. We obliged his request to exit the vehicle so he could do his job. He did a quick once around the Chevy and didn't see any noticeable damage, asking us to open the trunk so he could look inside. Bruce removed the two bags of luggage so he could get a better look. He clicked his pen into the "open" position and was checking off a few boxes on his clipboard.

"So far, so good," he said in a slight drawl. "Lemme get a look at the inside, will ya?"

He opened the driver's side door and sat in the seat, putting the key into the ignition and turning it a click. This lit the dashboard so he could get a better look at the odometer reading for his check sheet. He looked over his shoulder into the backseat to see if there was any damage and made some more checkmarks on his tally sheet.

When he got out of the car, he sounded more like a cowboy from the Old West than a dude from California. "Everything looks good, pardner. Lemme have your rental agreement, and you'll be on your way."

I reached into the open passenger window and snapped open the glove compartment latch, forgetting that we had carefully wedged it back into place so as not to draw any attention to it. The door came flying off, falling onto the floor of the car. Just then, a wide-eyed Mr. B grabbed the guy by the arm to distract him.

"Hey, Jake-ey pal, how long have you been working here?" he

said, trying to stall and make a little small talk, "You must meet a lot of chicks here, am I right?"

I snatched the paperwork and handed it to Catman, who passed it on to Jake. Then I reached down through the window to grab the compartment door from the floor and smack it in place. Too bad for the next guy trying to open that glove compartment.

He looked at our paperwork, handed me a copy of the inspection report, and said, "You're all set. Just bring this here report with ya to the gal at the desk. Have a great day now, ya hear?"

"Thanks, Tex," Mr. B shot back at him, pointing a "finger-gun" and pulling the imaginary trigger with his thumb. Jake gave him a smile and moseyed over to the next car.

With Bruce and Sal outside guarding the luggage and looking out for the airport tram, I headed inside to settle the bill. There were two people in front of me and only one reservation clerk. Waiting patiently for my turn, I noticed it was our old friend "Kelly," who had helped us when we first arrived. Although she didn't remember me, I certainly remembered her.

"Hey, Kelly. Nice to see you again," I said. "Do you remember me from last week?"

"I'm sorry, sir. Not really. What can I help you with tonight?" So much for making a lasting impression.

"Just returning our car. We're trying to make a nine o'clock flight, so we're in a little bit of a hurry."

"No problem, sir," she said as I handed her my rental agreement along with Jake's inspection report. "Everything looks good. I see that you have a credit for $15, so I'll take that off the final price."

"Thank you so much, Kelly," I smiled back at her. I turned around and saw Mr. B and the Catman standing outside the lobby window and gave them the "thumbs up" gesture. The Catman returned the universal "Big jugs" symbol, mimicking juggling two bowling balls. He then pointed to a chick waiting on the line behind me.

As usual, he was right.  She had a big rack.

"OK, that's nine days at $13.99 per day, a total of $125.91. Before I add the tax, let me take off..." I cut her off in mid-sentence.

"I'm sorry, did you say nine days?" I asked, "Today is Monday. We rented the car last Monday. We've only had the car eight days, Kelly."

"Yes sir," she stammered, "Any vehicle returned after 6 pm on the due date will be charged an additional day unless you arrange for a late return. It's in your contract."

"What are you talking about?" I asked through gritted teeth. "Our flight is not until 9 pm. Why would I need to bring the car back before 6 pm? That's ludicrous." I reached into my trusty folder for the original rental reservation voucher. "Here is my reservation voucher. The box for "Late Return" is checked and marked with my flight departure time of 9 pm."

Kelly looked carefully at the voucher and then at the rental agreement. "Sir, the voucher and the rental agreement seem to be different. Did you get a separate rental agreement when you came into LA?"

For a second, I didn't know how to answer that question. I took off my baseball hat and ran my fingers through my hair, trying to wrap my head around what she was saying. Just then, the Catman was tapping on the glass and pointing. The return van was pulling up to the curb. Mr. B had his palms up, indicating a silent "What's up?"

As the Catman loaded the bags onto the van, Mr. B sauntered into the lobby and said, "Disco, is there a problem here?"

"I hope not," I answered, as he joined me at the counter. I looked over to Kelly, who immediately made the connection and suddenly realized who she was dealing with again.

"Kelly," I said, "We were here on Monday and..."

"I remember now," she said. "Let me get Mr. Petchauer and see if he can straighten things out." She reached for the phone, whispered something into it, and Mr. Petchauer came out of the back room with a cup of coffee. It was the same manager we encountered on Monday. His nametag said, "Jimmy."

"What seems to be the..." he began, halting in mid-sentence as he recognized us almost immediately. "It's you guys!"

"That's right, Jack," Mr. B confirmed. "You better get this situation straightened out, or I'm going to shove my foot where the sun don't shine!"

Kelly handed the rental agreement to Jimmy and said, "Mr. P, there's no late arrival listed. I'm supposed to charge them for another day."

Before Mr. B could say another word, the Catman joined us and grabbed him to take him back outside. Of course, he really just wanted to get a better look at the chick on the line behind me.

"Look," I said, going into Good-Cop / Bad-Cop mode. "This is a simple mistake, right, Jimmy? When you gave us the new rental agreement, you just failed to check off the "Late Return" box on the agreement. Am I right Jimmy, pal?"

There were beads of sweat forming on his temples, and he loosened his yellow tie a little, unbuttoning the top button of this red shirt. "Yes, yes, of course," he said, handing the agreement back to Kelly a little shakily. "We'll take care of you, gentlemen. No problem."

Mr. Petchauer then reduced the number of rental days to 7, giving us a free day for our trouble. "Don't forget the $15 voucher, Kelly," I said with a smile. Our New York attitude had won again!

Jumping on the transportation van, we sped through the check-in process just as they were starting to board TWA flight 88 to Phoenix. Our seats were in the back of the plane, row 23, seats 4, 5, and 6. The Catman grabbed the window seat for the short flight.

We weren't operating on much sleep in the last 48 hours, so we all just closed our eyes and relaxed for the short flight. It's amazing how you get accustomed to flying after only a couple of times.

California had tried it's best to take us down, but we were up for the task. Like Rocky Balboa, we kept getting knocked down, but somehow made it back on our feet.

Now we were heading to Arizona to visit Bruce's friends from Long Island, Paul Kozshekka and Felix. They were in their final year at Arizona State University in Tempe. Although we didn't have any plans other than just staying with them for a couple of days, we knew one thing. It was going to be a full-out tardo couple of days. School started for them on Thursday, and we would be in full burn mode in Arizona.

Kozshekka grew up down the block from Bruce on Pittsburgh Avenue in Massapequa Park. I knew him from partying several times back on Long Island, but I had not met Felix before.

Paul was tall and lanky, almost a full head taller than everyone, with a real laid-back attitude. Nothing ever seemed to bother him. He always seemed surprised at things you told him, commenting, "Oh wow, man," or, "That's so cool!" The guy never seemed to have a bad word to say about anyone.

Growing up, Bruce told us Kozshekka had several nicknames, like "Koz" and "The H Man" because he loved laying around and being horizontal. He was the coolest dude I knew.

Maybe being so cool is what made him such a good pilot. He was studying aviation and had a pilot's license already. He often offered to take us up in a private plane to fly around Manhattan (you could rent one for the evening out of Republic Airport in Farmingdale on Long Island). Still, I could never do anything like that. Not because of him; I just couldn't ever see myself getting in a tiny plane under any circumstances, no matter who was in the pilot seat. Kozshekka enjoyed partying as much as the next guy, but when he was flying the next day, he knew the cutoff point and could just stop cold.

"This is going to be great," Bruce said as we walked through the Phoenix airport toward the Dollar Rent-A-Car desk. "I haven't seen Koz and Felix since last summer. They live in a two-bedroom Garden Apartment unit with a big living room and plenty of couch space. When I spoke to him, he said maybe we could go tubing on Tuesday."

"Are you sure about this tubing stuff?" I asked innocently.

"I'm telling you," he said, "You sit in a tire tube, then float down the river. It's about five hours of floating, drinking, smoking, and hanging out."

"And you've tubed before?"

"Of course. We went a few times while I was there for my only semester."

"And it's not dangerous?"

"No way, man," he said and then winked. "It's like riding a bus!" We both had a good laugh.

Surprisingly, we had no issues at all with the rental car in Phoenix. We got a light blue Chrysler LeBaron sedan with four doors. Before leaving the desk, I checked the rental agreement to make sure they checked the "Late Return" box. Our flight out of Phoenix was 11:30 pm.

While I was securing the car, Bruce grabbed a payphone to call Kozshekka and let him know we were on our way. He gave him the Reader's Digest version of the last 24 hours, including our "appearance" on *The Tonight Show*.

The LaCresenta apartments on Orange Avenue in Tempe were only about 10 miles from the Phoenix airport, so we made a quick stop at a convenience store to pick up two Styrofoam coolers and two cases of Heineken. Since we were staying for free with them, we wanted to show up with the good stuff.

We pulled into the resident parking lot about 11:30, and Kozshekka met us at the door with hugs and cold beers. "Hurry, man. It's on right now!" he said and pointed us to the living room, where Felix was already sitting.

Sure enough, we got inside just in time to hear the monologue joke, "There's still a newspaper strike in New York," followed by loud yelling from the audience. We saw Carson stop and turn away from the camera to look in the direction where we were sitting. Then he deadpanned, "Obviously some non-readers from New York," followed by the audience howling!

"That's so cool," Kozshekka said.

And he was right. It was cool.

"This calls for a celebration," Felix said, as he grabbed a joint from a little box on the table, lifting his beer, and making a toast, "Here's to the non-readers from New York!"

Felix was a lot shorter than Kozshekka (everyone was), and his long, thick, black hair was parted down the middle. He sported a '70s style mustache, wrapping slightly around his top lip. He resembled a Hispanic caricature. At first glance, I thought of "Cheech" Marin from the comedy duo of "Cheech and Chong." With all the smoking going on, it was hard not to make the comparison of Kozshekka with "Cheech's" partner, Tommy Chong. He was also a tall, lanky guy that always said things like, "Oh wow, man!"

We really weren't too interested in the rest of the show, so we turned down the TV sound and started listening to some music. We brought everyone up to speed on our trip so far, as we drank and smoked the night away.

"We have to go tubing tomorrow," Kozshekka pleaded, "It's great, and you just float through the river. We'll get stoned, bring beer and sandwiches, it'll be great!" So, we toasted to going tubing. Then we toasted to life in Arizona and toasted to Johnny Carson again. By the time we finished toasting, we were toasted.

Sometime around 1 am, the evening news was replaying on the TV. I saw the weather chick (blonde, of course) standing in front of the map and pointing to the Phoenix and Tempe area, where the graphic on the screen said it was currently 108 degrees.

108 degrees at night?

I had to go outside to see what 108 degrees felt like in the middle of the night. You know what? It wasn't too bad. It's a dry heat, you know.

The Catman and I found spots on the couch to crash for the evening, while Mr. B shacked up on the floor of Kozshekka's room and passed out. We all passed out.

We had two full days of partying ahead of us.

This was going to be the start of a foggy 48 hours; I could feel it...

# ARIZONA

# Arizona

Felix and Disco

Breakfast Buddies

Nice Hats!

Salt River

Trunk Beers

Felix and Mr. B

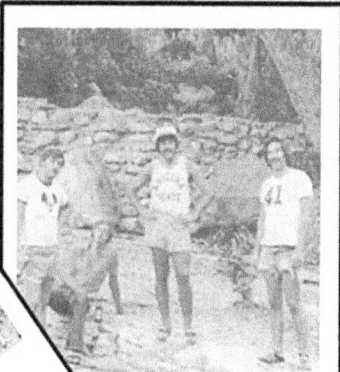

So, What?

# the Great Ice Heist

I woke up and stuck my head above the top of the couch to see what was going on in the kitchen behind me. Felix, Kozshekka, and Mr. B were up early and busy preparing for today's all-day burn. We were going tubing down the Salt River for a few hours, floating westward through the Tonto National Forest. "Salt River Tubing" would provide us with rental "tubes" for the day, but we needed to prepare our other supplies.

With military-like precision, everyone was taking care of business. Felix was cleaning some pot to extricate the seeds and twigs, packing it into a plastic zip-lock bag. Since we were going to be on the water, he also placed a pipe and two lighters into the baggie. It was essential to ensure the necessities were taken care of.

Kozshekka, meanwhile, was preparing an elaborate breakfast as Mr. B ventured outside to stockpile the adult refreshments. There were some ice cubes leftover from last night, but it was barely enough for the smaller cooler, which we would take with us on the river. The larger beer-keeper, which required much more ice, was needed for the trunk so we could enjoy a few during the over two-hour drive to the Salt Lake, but we would solve that dilemma later.

With the Catman still asleep across from me on the other side of the couch, I put my head back down to catch a couple of extra zzz's. I closed my eyes and was just beginning to nod off when I heard Springeteen's "Thunder Road" coming from the radio in the kitchen. Suddenly, there was a pipe being shoved into my mouth.

"Good morning, sunshine!" Mr. B grinned as I opened one eye to see what was happening. Without hesitation, he lit the pipe and said, "Bomb's away!"

Just another day in paradise.

As I made my way into the kitchen, Kozshekka was already putting the finishing touches on his famous scrambled eggs and bacon. The toast was optional. When I asked why they were famous, he smiled and said, "I add my own special sauce to them." I never found out what exactly was in the sauce, but being it was Arizona, I'm sure it had something to do with hot sauce. He spiked a sampling of his creation onto a fork and held it in front of my face, saying like a proud papa feeding his infant, "Open wide!" The eggs were surprisingly fluffy and, not surprisingly, very spicy.

Popping some bread into the toaster, I made myself a plate and sat next to Felix as he sipped his morning coffee. "This is going to be great, man," he said as he reached for the schnapps and added it to his morning brew. "You want some?"

I wasn't much of a coffee drinker, but when in Rome...

Felix and Kozshekka had multiple pairs of sneakers, some specifically for tubing. "You gotta wear shoes in the water, man," Kozshekka said as he put a second pair into a bag. We, on the other hand, had packed enough clothes for the entire West Coast trip, but only one pair of sneakers. Felix insisted that just an hour or two in the sun tomorrow, and they would be dry.

After breakfast, I put on a t-shirt and bathing suit for our day in the water. I was convinced this was going to fuck up my sneakers, regardless of how quickly they dried.

When the doorbell rang, Felix was elbow deep in his egg breakfast and asked me to open the door. "It's our friends Diane and Kate," he said in a slight mumble before swallowing. "They're coming tubing with us."

Diane was a short, light-haired brunette with an oval face and beautiful blue eyes. Kate was a shapely dark-haired beauty with a "perky" athletic build. The Catman would have noted she had perky, well, you know what the Catman would have said by now. Both wore jean shorts and tank tops over their bathing suits.

Previously dead to the world, the Catman instinctively knew there were females in the room and sprang to attention (in more ways than one). Both were very cordial to me at first glance, but Kate soared past me and gave Mr. B a huge hug. Apparently, there was some familiarity between them that I was unaware of. "I don't tell you everything, you know," he admitted later.

Even though we could squeeze all six of us into our Chrysler, we still needed a second car once we got to the Salt River. The distance between the starting and endpoints of the tubing run was about 10 miles. When you finished the run, you needed a way to get back to the starting point, where the other car is parked.

The plan was to meet at the endpoint, where we would leave Felix's car for the return trip later. We would then pile into the LeBaron and drive to the starting point. When we were done, we would pack everyone into Felix's car and drive back to the start, where the LeBaron would be waiting. Easy, peasy.

It was almost 11 o'clock by the time we were completely locked and loaded. Diane and Kate rode with Felix while Kozshekka tagged along with us. We had everything we needed for our all-day burn except the ice for the big cooler. I casually asked where we should stop to get the ice.

"Oh, we're not buying ice, man." Kozshekka deadpanned. "We're appropriating it!"

Appropriating it?

"We have a place we can get it for free," Felix offered. "Just follow me."

Our first stop was the "Vagabond Motel" on Apache Boulevard, not far from the apartment. "They have an ice machine outside in the breezeway," Felix explained. "We'll pull into the parking lot and fill the cooler with ice. But we need to be discreet, so we don't get caught. The office manager is a chubby little guy that can be a real dick sometimes."

"Have you guys gotten caught before?" I asked.

"Of course," laughed Kozshekka. "But, we can usually outrun the dude!"

The parking lot was all gravel. Many of the parking areas we found in Arizona were made of gravel or dirt. Other than the roads, there weren't a lot of blacktopped open spaces due to the heat they generate. Even from inside the air-conditioned Chrysler, you could feel the midday heat rising off the gravel in the parking lot. We followed the dusty entrails of Felix's tires that led us to the breezeway.

The connected motel rooms of the Vagabond stretched single file, lined up away from the office, which anchored the property near the main road. The white stucco walls required a proper power washing as the light green moss was beginning to take over. The trim, which was once a pretty blue, looked like it was at least five years past its due date. There was a five-foot-wide cement walkway connecting all the units that were protected by an extended roof, providing what little shade it could.

A smattering of cars were parked neatly in front of a few blue doors. Each door was adorned with an identifying number, starting with "101," nearest the office, and stretching chronologically outward to the end, where number "121" stood without any vehicle accompaniment. Like most public venues, the owners of the Vagabond must have been superstitious or at least assumed their guests might be. I noticed there was no blue door with "113" on the front. The breezeway was located between units "112" and "114," presumably a small common area containing coin-operated soda and snack machines for the customers. According to Felix, this is also where our target ice machine was located.

As we followed Felix into the parking lot, the DJ on the radio teased a Springsteen song right after the break. "You know what that means!" Mr. B beamed.

Felix pulled over by the breezeway, and Diane got out to get some more ice for her cooler. Felix pointed to the deserted area down towards door "121" and said, "Let's go over there and wait," as he headed out.

With Kozshekka and Bruce in the back seat preparing for the mandatory "Springsteen Burn," the Catman, riding shotgun, was designated for ice detail. I shut off the engine and handed him the keys. The ignition key was the same as the trunk key, and we only had one of those.

"May The Force be with you," I smiled, as he headed out the door.

He grabbed the cooler, closed the trunk, and flipped the keys back to me. I started the car and headed to the rendezvous spot. "Meet us over there," I told the Catman, pointing to where Felix was.

"Back in a sec," he answered.

Just then, Springsteen's "Badlands" came on the radio. Kozshekka and Bruce just smiled and lit the fuse.

I moved the vehicle over to the far end of the parking lot, but since it was made of gravel and a little uneven, hit a bump or two along the way, causing the trunk to open. I guess the Catman didn't close it all the way.

"Mother fucker," I said when we came to a stop, backing the car up, so we had a clear view of the entire property. I was going to close it, but since it was now my turn to take a hit, I said, "Fuck it. Now I don't have to open it again!"

We were close enough to pass the bowl between the open car windows while we waited. Diane had filled her small cooler and returned to Felix's car, but Catman was nowhere to be seen. "I think he's talking to someone," Diane said.

When the song was over, the Catman still hadn't popped back out of the vestibule. Just then, we heard someone yelling, "Hey, come back with that! That's for customers only!!"

We saw the Catman moving quickly with the cooler and some fat guy chomping on a cigar standing outside the main office flailing his arms. Now he was waddling toward the Catman and trying to pick up the pace. He was failing miserably. I put it into gear with the trunk wide open to rendezvous with the Catman. I stopped in front of door number "114" and jumped out to give him a hand. For some reason, he had a piece of paper folded in his mouth. He mumbled something as I grabbed the cooler from him and threw it into the open trunk, slamming it closed and checking it to make sure it was appropriately secured.

He jumped back into the passenger seat and slammed the door. "I got that chick's number," he beamed as he opened the paper to show us the name, "Julia," with a little heart over the letter "I."

"She's here with some of her friends, and they're having a party tonight."

"Works for me," I said, gunning the engine and heading for the exit, expecting Felix to do the same. Instead, he headed toward the little fat guy, who was doubled over and catching his breath. He barely made it to door "108."

"Can I help you with something?" Felix said, grinning from ear to ear. Full of sweat and breathing heavily, the guy was just about to open his mouth when Felix gunned it, leaving him surrounded in a cloud of dust and gravel.

The pudgy motel manager pinwheeled and was now looking directly at us. I followed Felix's lead, leaving my own trail of gravel and dust. You could see him through the back window stamping his feet and waving his little arms.

# the Salt River of Death

It was about a two-hour drive to get to "Salt River Tubing" from Tempe. Just before hitting State Road 87, we pulled over and grabbed a few beers from the trunk. You really couldn't be driving a car with a cooler full of beer on the back seat. If you got pulled over, you'd be fucked. Instead, we had to periodically pull over and grab a few cold ones from the trunk, then continue onward.

We met up with Felix and the girls at the ending point of the tube run off Bush Highway. Felix would leave his car there, and when we finished tubing, we would all pile into his car for the ride back to the starting point, where our car would be. Transferring everything and everyone into our vehicle made for a cramped trip to the starting point.

As Felix was closing his trunk and locking his car, I noticed the large key ring he was carrying. "Who are you, Schneider from *One Day at a Time?*" I asked, referencing the janitor from the popular

TV series. "No, man," he said, "I have keys for everything on here. My apartment, my stash box, work. I even have two sets of keys for the car in case I lose one."

I was sorry I asked…

Diane sat in between Catman and me in the front seat, while Felix and Kate piled into the back with Mr. B and Kozshekka. Kate sat on Mr. B's lap. When I looked at him through the rear-view mirror, he had a smile on his face that would have made The Catman proud.

Once we disembarked at the starting point and rented our tubes, we added two additional ones for the coolers. There was a beautiful open "rest" area about half-way down the river route with a few tables. Riders would get out of their tubes in the shallow water and walk over to the shore, where they could take a break and hang out on dry land.

Felix, Kozshekka, and the girls had done this run several times, but this was the first time Sal and I had ever done anything like this, so we were looking to them for advice.

"First and foremost," said Kozshekka, "You have to protect the beer, man." The beer cooler had a lead rope that someone would tie to their tube, so it didn't float away. The tire used for that was smaller so the ice chest would fit more snuggly in it. Instead of a big open hole in the middle, there was a mesh "bottom," so whatever you wanted to put into the opening wouldn't really dip far below the surface of the water, as your ass would.

During the four-hour trip, Kozshekka would have the beer floating along with him on a leash to keep it within arm's reach. Diane took responsibility for the other cooler. When you wanted a beer or soda, you floated over to the cooler and grabbed one. When you were finished, you just put the empties back in the cooler.

Our floating tubes were repurposed innertubes from giant truck tires. You went into the shallow starting area, just a few feet off the shore, and stuck your ass in the hole with your back against one side and your legs sticking out over the other end. There was a slight trick to getting into the tube. Standing in the shallow water, you jumped up and plopped in. Once comfortably seated, you used your hands as paddles and moved into deeper water, towards the middle of the river, and into the current.

The Salt River wound its way through Tonto National Forest westward past Tempe and into Phoenix. It was a fantastic experience. You didn't have to know where you were going because there was only one way to go, wherever the current was taking you.

What we didn't know was that the current was going to take us for a ride that we weren't expecting.

---

I was about balls deep in the surprisingly warm and crystal blue water as we grabbed our innertubes and waded out in the shallows away from the shore. Without ever having floated in a tube before, I turned to watch the others get into theirs so I could mimic the procedure. Kozshekka grabbed his tube and positioned it behind him, then launched himself into the air, falling gently back into it. The girls were already settled butt deep into theirs. Mr. B sprang into his tube just like a pro, and the Catman followed suit.

I put the tube into position behind me, launched into the air, and came down ass first in the water. When I turned, my tire was sneaking away down the river and following the current. "Your tube is downstream from your ass," Kozshekka said, "You have to be downstream from the tube, man!"

That made sense.

I chased after it and switched positions. Standing downstream from the tube didn't seem to help me. It was still trying to maneuver around me to follow the current as if it had a mind of its own. I launched into the air again, but came up short and, once again, landed ass first in the water to the delight of everyone.

"And the Russian judge gives him a 2.5," Mr. B yelled, while everyone laughed.

This time, Kozshekka got out of his tube and headed in my direction, dragging the beer cooler right behind. "Can I help you, little boy?" he said with a huge smile as he held my tube for me. I was able to get inside without further issues,

"Here's your reward!" he said, reeling in the beer cooler and grabbing a cold Coors. He popped the top and said, "The pause that refreshes!"

We grouped ourselves together after a few minutes, locking our legs together and forming a circle with the beer and soda coolers in the middle. This seemed to be the favorite position of most groups we spied on the river. Part of the beauty of the float was the undisturbed scenery. The Salt River was carved between rock formations with an eerie resemblance to otherworldly science fiction movies.

Surrounded by orange cliffs, I felt like Captain Kirk and his landing party on Mars. The lines etched in the stone walls told the story of millions of years of erosion, reminding you of the power of flowing water. The current was moving so slowly, we almost didn't notice we were moving at all.

After sharing a bowl or two and a round of beers, we broke formation and began floating on our own. Kozshekka made an announcement, seeking anyone who wanted a fresh beer. I was feeling pretty toasty at the time, so I declined.

Laying on my back in the tube, I closed my eyes and enjoyed the warm sun projecting shades of red through my eyelids. Based on the partying we'd done in the last 48 hours and the lack of sleep, it would have been easy to catch a few zzz's while we were floating.

"Oh man, I forgot to tell you," Kozshekka offered as he broke the awed silence of a very stoned group of people. "There are parts of the river with rock formations just under the surface. Most of us know where they are by now. Whenever we get close, someone will yell, 'asses up' as a warning. That means we need to pick our asses up out of the tube, or you are going to get bounced."

Just then, almost on cue, someone a few yards in front of us yelled, "ASSES UP!"

I saw Kozshekka lift his ass out of the water a few inches. Soon, the others were sliding their asses out, almost laying horizontal on top of the tube. Being a newbie, I only lifted my derrière up a little. The unseen rock grazed my cheeks a little, but caused no real damage. I felt it nonetheless, reminding myself to heed those warnings in the future.

Most of the trip was in the direct sun, although our decision to take an afternoon journey instead of an early morning journey helped, as the sun was no longer directly over us. I learned quickly to keep my tire cool by splashing water over the sides every now and then to alleviate the incredible heat building up on the rubber. Moving your leg or arm over a hot tube is a burning experience.

Periodically, you splashed yourself like an Elephant from Africa, cooling the top of your head, upper body, and legs as you went along. On this trip, the only thing waterlogged was your ass. Where the water was shallow, you could jump out and do a complete cool down. I got to be an expert at getting back into the tube after the first few miles.

During the float, I asked Kozshekka if there was a bathroom area along the route. "What for, man?" he replied as if I had asked him why the sky was blue. "As long as you don't need to go number two, you just kinda go."

Fascinating.

It took some time before I perfected the "piss and swim" technique. After a few tries, it became quite pleasurable. Of course, since you were moving at the same speed as the water, you couldn't stay inside your tube and relieve yourself, that would be disgusting. To avoid sitting in your own piss, when the water was deep enough, you would move your legs down inside the tube with you, draping your arms over the top, like you were standing up. That way, you could "relieve yourself" under the surface of the water.

You could always tell what someone was doing based on their position in the tube, along with a sly smile of relief. As disgusting as this might sound, it was socially acceptable for both men and women. After all, when you gotta go, you gotta go.

The width of the river's crystal blue water varied from narrow to a few hundred yards in each direction. Even the landscape changed every few minutes as we floated by. We went from the Sahara Desert to the riverbanks of the Old West. Tumbleweeds were blowing across deserted areas dotted with cacti, while others were rich with foliage. At times, we were close enough to read the license plates of cars on the Bush Highway, while other areas seemed foreign and desolate. Huge hills jutted out at times for no reason, revealing eons of wear and tear. Although there was a sparse amount of brush available, some areas had no real relief from the beating sun and the desert sand.

As we made our way to an open spot, just outside of the primary current, we jumped out of our tubes and waded to the shoreline. The sandy beach was made up mostly of small rocks, but it was too hot to sit on. Instead, we pulled our tubes up on the shore and sat in the shallow water. Felix went swimming to cool off, and most of us followed him.

We relaxed on the shore and ate the sandwiches and snacks the girls had prepared. Although we were just floating, the hot sun was beginning to take its toll. This was the most relaxed I had been on the entire trip, and the heat was sapping my strength.

We passed around the pipe and just enjoyed the scenery.

After about a half-hour, we grabbed our now steaming tubes, cooled them in the water, and then jumped in to continue our journey. We had been floating, drinking, and smoking for more than three hours. I would have been just as happy to walk over to the main road, hail a cab, and call it a day. I think the sun was baking my brain. Both Mr. B and the Catman looked a little like "Larry the Lobster," so I knew I couldn't be that far behind them.

"The pace is going to pick up a bit, boys and girls," Kozshekka warned as we drifted back into the current. "We have to get through a few hundred yards of white-water, but it's no big deal, man. We've done it a bunch of times."

Funny, I don't remember any talk about white-water in any discussions we had before getting my ass into this tube. Every description of this adventure included the word "float." Somehow, I had a feeling it was going to be a big deal, after all.

After about 15 minutes of floating at a brisker pace (and a few more "Asses up!" callouts), we suddenly heard the flow of the water for the first time, Ahead, we could see a slight bend in the river. As the groups in front of us passed the curve, they dipped, resembling the lead cars on a roller coaster from your view in the last car. The river was heading around the bend and dropping a few feet, causing the water to speed up, almost like a small waterfall. You could now see a spray coming from the river.

As the water roared around him, Felix, who was ahead of the group, yelled, "HERE WE GO!" and dropped out of sight around the bend,

I looked at the Catman, and he was grabbing hold of the tube, so I did the same. As we came around the bend, the river dipped a few feet, and suddenly we were in a rushing rapid like you see in the movies. With my heart trying to escape through my throat, I clung to the tube and steered into the rapids. I was being tossed left and right, trying to maintain my balance, always leaning in the opposite direction the river wanted me to go, Suddenly, I wasn't having fun anymore.

Out of the corner of my eye, I saw Bruce get flipped over and separated from his tube. Felix and Kozshekka were arm-paddling to the shore to help Bruce as he drifted over there. Kozshekka was able to grab Bruce while Felix grabbed his tube to keep it from going down the river alone.

I looked around and saw the girls calmly making their way to the other side of the riverbank with their cooler. Unfortunately, the beer cooler trailing Kozshekka ran into a rock formation under the surface of the water and spilled over. All the remaining beer was gone.

Turning around to look behind me, I couldn't find Sal at all, not even his tube. Over the roar of the rapids, I heard someone call to me, but I couldn't make out what they were saying. Unfortunately, they were yelling, "ASSES UP!"

With the rushing water turning my tube around, I was facing the wrong direction, looking behind me instead of in front. I never saw the rock formation until it was too late, The tube struck the rock, turned on its side, and I was airborne.

The water was racing all around me, grabbing with unseen fingers and preventing me from thinking straight. Being dragged under for a few seconds, I got back to the surface and grabbed the edge of my tube. I couldn't touch the bottom, so I couldn't propel myself back inside. It was like treading water in the deep end of a swimming pool, only I was being rocketed down the river by the current. Now we were both at the mercy of the raging current without any control over direction. The tube was leading me right into a rock jutting above the surface, so I had to let it go and swim my way around the obstruction.

With nothing to buoy me above the water anymore, I went under again and realized that I had no control over the situation. The water was moving too fast for me to swim against it, and I couldn't reach the bottom. Cresting the surface like a desperate humpback whale, I snatched another quick breath before being drawn under again.

This was it; I was sure. This was how it was going to end.

The inflated truck-size innertube that obediently floated me into this mess was now racing solo in the same direction as me, but just outside of my reach. Right behind it were two other empty tires, presumably having dumped their former occupants as well.

I spied Bruce, Kozshekka, and Felix, signaling for me to swim across the current to where they were. I was always a good swimmer, but this was more like riding a wave at the beach, only you never actually reach the beach. The ride is powerful and out of your control, with no end in sight.

Steering to rocks protruding from the shoreline, I grabbed one and held on. Unfortunately, the undercurrent insisted on carrying the bottom half of my body down the river, with or without me. I fought against it, only to dip under again as the slippery rocks provided no gripping surface.

I emerged again, but this time I could touch the river bottom. I was close enough to the shore where my friends were located and grabbed onto another set of rocks, nestling inside them so I could catch my breath. I could hear them yelling and cheering as they jumped in the water to help me, only I wasn't in any mood to celebrate.

Our tubes slowly drifted into a little ebb of water just outside the rapids, including our now empty beer-tube. The girls made their way across the river to meet us. Of course, the Catman was with the girls on the other side, why wouldn't he be?

"That was wild, man!" Kozshekka said, as I scrambled up the rock and walked over to the riverbed. I sat down to take inventory and do a damage report, but everything was in working order. Just then, Mr. B came over, put his arm around me, and said, "You need this," handing me the pipe and flipping on the flame from the lighter.

And he was right. It was more frightening than dangerous, I guess. I was fighting in the rapids, but in less than 100 yards, I was going to be in calmer waters again. The girls were able to salvage a few of the beers, so we shared them and buried the empties in the sand before we got back into the tubes to finish the run down the river.

Although I had enjoyed this vacation on the West Coast, I was ready to go home. Unfortunately, the West Coast wasn't finished with us just yet.

# the Good Guys vs. the Tractor Trailer

We floated quietly and peacefully over the final hour or so without incident, reaching the shallow water at the ending point. Having my feet touch the river bottom in waist-deep water was oddly comforting. Once on shore, we trudged through the exit area to return our tubes.

Making our way out of the return building, we were greeted with the beginnings of a beautiful sunset. This was the end of a remarkable all-day burn. We had consumed a good portion of the beer before the rapids took their toll, but that was more than an hour ago.

We had towels and some nosh items in the car, but more importantly, we had enough foresight to have a cooler of beer waiting in the trunk. We still had a long ride ahead of us with not a lot of places to stop along the way.

What we didn't have were the car keys.

"That's not cool, man," exclaimed Kozshekka as he saw Felix frantically searching through every pocket he had.

"I'm telling you, dude, I don't have them," Felix said.

"You gotta have them, man," Kozshekka responded, "I don't fucking have them!"

"You had them when we left the parking lot, Felix," Kate said. "I saw you take them with you. You were dangling them around your finger like a prison warden."

We all met at the ending point, where we were now stranded with Felix's Ford Granada. We needed his car to drive back up to the starting point to retrieve our Chrysler.

"There were like 10 keys on that ring, man," Felix admitted. "I couldn't put them in my pock…" and he stopped in mid-sentence and pointed at me, "Shit, I think I left them in your car!"

"Looks like we gotta hitch a ride back to the top, my friend," Felix said, looking at me. Then he looked at one end of the parking lot and said, "You go that way, I'll go this way. See if someone can give us a lift. They all goin' back that way anyway, right?"

The problem was most cars were filled with people doubling up in one car. I asked a few people, but no one had room for two extra people. Just then, Felix was yelling across the parking lot, "Hey man, give me your keys. I got a dude that can squeeze me in."

I flipped him the keys. "If I can't find my keys," he said, "We'll all drive back in your car and then come back tomorrow and pick up my car."

The ride back to the starting point was at least 10 miles away, and the parking lot was becoming deserted. We waited for Felix to return, not knowing if he would have car keys or not. The Western sky was beginning to bleed reds and purples.

"I could hotwire this thing if I had to," Mr. B boasted, as he leaned on the hood of Felix's car, talking to Kate. I think she was buying his bullshit.

"When did you ever hotwire a car?" I interjected.

"My old man showed me how to do it years ago," he replied, looking directly at Kate as if I weren't there. "He was always fiddling with cars. He should have been a mechanic. And if there is one thing he loved, it was Fords."

I could see that old Eddie Haskell gleam in his eye. There was no possible way he could hotwire a car...

Felix returned triumphantly with our LeBaron and was dangling the magic keyring out the window. Guess we'll never know if Mr. B could really hotwire a car. We bid farewell to Felix and the girls and told them we would meet them later.

As we headed west on the two-lane SR 87, we were making good time despite a couple of stops to retrieve beer from the trunk and relieve ourselves. We decided to coordinate the two events next time we needed to stop. Soon, we came across a big rig that was moving way too slow for our liking. We spent almost 20 minutes behind the behemoth without any suitable opportunities, or straight roads, to make our move around it.

"This guy is driving like a hoople-i-tis" Mr. B boomed, as he took a hit from the joint, making its way around the inside of the car.

"Not much we can do about it," I answered.

"I think we have a straightaway coming up in a mile or two," Kozshekka chimed in, "We can pass there, I'm positive."

I kept my eye out for the straightaway, and sure enough, there it was, right up ahead. You could see the solid yellow line on our side break into dashes. I briefly thought about naming Kozshekka my new Navigational Specialist, but decided against it.

With no oncoming traffic in sight, I put the pedal to the metal and began picking up speed, racing out into the oncoming traffic lane. Soon we were beeping the horn and giving the driver the finger as we speed past him and into the twilight.

The celebration in the car was joyous, and Bruce announced, "That calls for a round of beers!"

"Oh wow, man," Kozshekka said, "All the beers are in the trunk."

"If we have to get the beer out of the trunk," I reminded everyone, "I need to stop the car and shut off the engine. It's the same key."

Shit, we hadn't thought about that. Bummer.

"I got an idea," I blurted out. "How long do you think it would take to stop the car, grab the beer and get back into the car?"

"One minute and thirty-seven seconds," Mr. B blurted out.

"How the fuck would you know that?" the Catman asked.

"How do you know it's NOT one minute at thirty-seven seconds?" Mr. B asked back.

That began a discussion and planning session that would change the course of all our lives forever. Just kidding, but it did require timing and coordination.

We picked up speed and began to put some distance between us and the rig. It was impossible to know how far in front we actually were because of the curves in the road. While I was concentrating on getting us enough lead time, the geniuses in the back seat were developing our plan.

The key for the trunk was the same as the ignition. We would need a long stretch of straight road to pull over, shut off the engine, open the trunk, grab a few beers, and get back on the road—all before the truck caught up with us. Like General Patton preparing an enemy attack, a plan was hatched.

As we organized our manpower, each person was assigned a specific task based on where they were sitting in the car. The plan was simple. I had the ignition keys, so I opened the trunk. Kozshekka, in the back seat on the driver's side, and Mr. B next to him, would grab the beers. The Catman, riding shotgun, was the lookout and trunk closer.

The sequencing of events was crucial. I would pull the car onto the shoulder, grab the key out of the ignition, and race to the trunk to open it. Once the trunk was open, I jump back into the driver's seat and restart the car. To make sure I wouldn't crash into Kozshekka's door in the back, he would wait for me to pass him before opening his door, then follow me to the trunk. At the same time, Mr. B exits his door, heading to the back of the car. Both back doors would be left open because when they returned, their hands would be filled with beer cans. The Catman would race behind Bruce and keep his eyes peeled on the road behind us as a lookout for that truck. As soon as the boys had their loot, his responsibility was to close the cooler and the trunk.

Of course, this was predicated on completing all those tasks before the truck appeared and passed us. We weren't getting stuck behind it again. After all, when we passed the rig on the road, we beeped and gave the driver the finger. I had a strong feeling he was going to remember that.

The plan, which took much longer than it should have to develop, was flawless. Now we just had to execute it.

We were pumped.

We were psyched.

We were ready.

Unfortunately, we were also very stoned.

Just around the next curve, we came upon a long straightaway. I gunned it down the road as we all strained our necks looking behind us, confirming there was no sign of the Semi. Coming to the end of the straightaway, I yelled, "This is IT!" and jammed on the breaks, steering the car onto the gravelly shoulder.

I slammed the car into park, took a deep breath and shouted, "LET'S DO THIS, MOTHER FUCKERS!" and grabbed the ignition key, jumping out of the car into the night. Catman then jumped out of the car, only to get smashed by Mr. B's door as he opened it into his body. Laughing like lunatics, Mr. B and Kozshekka raced to the back of the car, but I was struggling to get the trunk open.

Then, like something from a Stephen King novel, the headlights of the Semi appeared from behind the curve. "IT'S COMING!" the Catman yelled.

I gave it another wiggle, and the trunk finally flew open. I rushed back to the driver's seat and started the car. I could see the Semi was bearing down on us, so this was going to be close.

With their arms full of beer, Kozshekka and Bruce headed back to the car. Unfortunately, Mr. B went ass over tea kettle in the gravel on the shoulder with beers flying everywhere. A few cans of Coors were spitting small streams into the air like broken fire hydrants.

The truck was getting closer.

Bruce ran to salvage a few that didn't open. "Forget them!" I yelled as I could see the truck closing fast.

Meanwhile, the Catman was standing behind the car with the trunk still open. "Close that trunk!" I screamed out the window. "We have to get out of here right fucking now!"

Catman grabbed a few beers himself and slammed the trunk closed. Mr. B scrambled onto his feet and jumped back into the car headfirst. This was going to be close.

"LET'S GO, LET'S GO, MAN!" Kozshekka was shouting as Mr. B face-planted into the back of the car, then scrambled to reach out and grab the door..

"GO, GO, GO, GO, GO!" they all shouted as I began spinning the tires in the gravel before Mr. B even had a chance to close his door. When the tires finally made solid contact, we shot out onto the road just in front of the approaching truck. We could hear the air brakes of the 18-wheeler whistling as we positioned ourselves in front of the hard-charging 15,000-pound vehicle and began pulling away from it. Now he was blasting his air horn and sticking a handgun out the window!

Oh wait, he was just giving us the finger.

To celebrate this most triumphant moment, Kozshekka lit up a bowl, and we all participated, even the Catman. Mr. B looked at his watch and announced, "One minute and thirty-seven seconds, just like I said."

"Oh wow, man," Kozshekka remarked. "We forgot to take a piss." We still had about 30 miles to go, but we weren't going to do that again. Everyone was going to have to wait until we got back to Tempe.

Mr. B distributed his beers to Kozshekka and me, and I put mine between my legs on the driver's seat as it was my turn to take a hit from the bowl. When I was done, I reached down into my crotch and opened the beer, which began spraying all over me.

"FUUUUUCCKKK!" I yelled while everyone else had a good laugh.

"Oh man, this is bullshit," I said to Bruce. "Is this one of the fucking cans you dropped?"

"Maybe, maybe not," he said as he smiled that Eddie Haskill grin again. "Only one way to find out. Beer Roulette! Everyone put the can up to your face and open it. No bullshitting or chickening out."

Kozshekka was the first to go. He held the beer up to his nose, closed his eyes, and popped the top, then was showered in foam. The Catman was next and grabbed one from his stash. "This is fucked," he said as he lined up the can to his face, closed his eyes in anticipation, and popped the cap. No spray!

"Of course not, you dickwads," he said, laughing. "I didn't drop mine."

That left just Bruce. "You better do it, man," Kozshekka threatened. Mr. B held up the beer to his face and grabbed the pop-top. I noticed it was covered in road dirt and was probably one of the beers he dropped. This was going to squirt like a fire hose.

"I'm no pussy," he said, "Let's count it down, shall we? Three, two, one!"

But instead of popping the top and taking his beer shower, he pointed the beer at Catman's head and said, "BOOM," opening the can and showering the Catman instead. We all roared with laughter.

"Who's a dickwad now, Catman!"

I took one look at the Catman, who was wiping the beer off his glasses, and we knew what we had to do. He looked at Kozshekka with a smile and said, "On Three. One, Two, Three!" And we all shook our beers and pointed them at Mr. B. All was right with the world again.

Things settled down after a few minutes, and we got back to the mundane task of driving home on a darkened highway. When we got home, I was toast. I don't think I had ever been so exhausted. We took turns taking showers while waiting for the pizza guy. Although Felix and Kozshekka had gotten used to Arizona pizza, it's just not the same outside of New York. Not that I was complaining; we were all hungry.

The Catman decided to meet up with Julia, the girl he met from the motel during the Great Ice Heist, but I just wasn't up for it. I needed to crash, so I went into Kozshekka's room and fell asleep on the floor. Mr. B and Kate disappeared for an hour or two while Kozshekka, Felix, and Diane hung out in the living room.

I got up around 2 am to pee and found the Catman passed out on the couch. I didn't see Mr. B yet, so I curled up on the other couch. I heard him come in about an hour later and head to Kozshekka's room.

Our red-eye flight back to New York was not until 11:30 pm tomorrow, so we had the whole day Wednesday to hang out and do it all again.

I think I'm going to need a vacation when I get back home…

# the Last Day Begins

My body hurt.

I had a pretty good sunburn from tubing the Salt River yesterday, as did everyone, but all my muscles hurt. Maybe being banged around in the whitewater of the river yesterday was taking its toll.

Rolling off the couch like a walrus, I struggled to my feet and sauntered into the bathroom to pee. I found aspirin in the medicine cabinet, hoping it would alleviate my soon-to-be raging headache.

It was a little after nine, and everyone was still asleep. We were taking the redeye out of Phoenix at 11:30 tonight, arriving back in New York early in the morning. In less than 24 hours, our West Coast adventure would be over.

I took it upon myself to make the coffee and get breakfast ready, but the cupboard was bare. This was going to require a quick trip to the supermarket. It was the least I could do for our hosts, Kozshekka and Felix. After getting dressed, I slipped on my sneakers before heading out. Unfortunately, they were still a little soggy and I squished my way out the door.

The car stunk to high heaven after the beer showers from the ride home last night. I opened all the windows and drove around the neighborhood a few times, airing the car out. I picked up supplies for breakfast, including two more cases of beer. Although the sun was shining, the radio DJ indicated we might get some rain in the afternoon. I figured we could use a "down" day anyway, so I also sprang for cold cuts and rolls to make lunch.

When returning to the apartment, there were still no signs of life. I shucked out of my sneakers and took Felix's advice, placing them outside in the direct sunlight. Once back inside, I figured out the mechanics of the coffee machine and got organized for breakfast. As soon as the bacon was frying, the corpses began springing back to life.

"You got the coffee going, man," Felix commented, making his way into the kitchen. "It smells good! I think I'm having it straight today. No booze, my head hurts." I pointed to the almost finished drip pot and smiled.

"You da man, Disco!" he laughed, "Hey, that was some day yesterday, right?"

"One I'll never forget," I told him. "I'm taking individual egg orders today, my friend. What can I do you for?"

"Ooooohh," he answered. "Let's do over easy, with toast and bacon on the side." He headed for the coffee machine and waited patiently while the last bit dripped into the pot.

Just then, Mr. B made an appearance. He had on a tank top and shorts that looked like they were slept in. His hair was pointing in all directions, but mostly north. "Nice hat!" I commented about his hair. "Have you looked in the mirror, yet?"

"Should I?" he replied.

"I wouldn't," I advised.

He looked at me and I asked him what he wanted, pointing out the various options with my trusty spatula. "No eggs, man," he said grabbing some bread for the toaster. "I'm in bad shape today."

"Join the club," I replied. "What happened to you last night?" I asked, as if I didn't know.

"We had a good time, I think," he said. "When I got back, you guys were dead to the world."

He joined Felix at the table after his toast popped. I scrambled myself some eggs with cheese, added bacon, and threw it inside a roll with ketchup before joining them with a cup of coffee. I think I'm beginning to like this coffee thing in the morning.

Kozshekka and the Catman joined us after a while and I jumped back into my role as chef for the morning.

"Oh wow, man," Kozshekka noted as he looked around the cupboard and fridge. "You made a run this morning for supplies! Very cool. Thanks, man."

The Catman opted for orange juice instead of coffee. Soon, Felix was lighting a joint and passing it around. "I didn't hear a Springsteen song," the Catman mumbled.

"Springsteen song?" Felix replied in an over-the-top Spanish accent, like the bandits from the movie *The Treasure of the Sierra Madre*, "We don't need no stinkin' Springsteen song!"

It's going to be just another foggy day in Arizona, I guess.

By lunchtime, it was getting cloudy outside and we were hurting buckaroos, so we decided to just hang home. I ran outside to grab my sneakers and close the windows on the car before the sun completely disappeared. Soon, it was raining lightly, but the real heavy stuff wasn't supposed to happen until overnight. We hadn't seen rain the entire trip.

The Catman regaled us with his story from the night before, although to this day, I still don't believe him. "There were five of them," he said with a gleam in his eye. "You guys all should have come, there was one for each of you!"

"You're telling me you had sex with five chicks?" Mr. B inquired.

"I didn't have sex with all of them," Catman replied with that Cheshire cat smile. "Some of them were having sex with each other. I was just happy to be in the middle!"

We spent the afternoon sitting in the living room, listening to music, smoking, and having a few beers. My body couldn't take much more abuse, so I participated more like a lightweight. There were lots of laughs during that afternoon, and it was just what the doctor ordered. Some rest and relaxation.

The plan was to have dinner at a nice steakhouse in Phoenix, located a few hundred yards from the airport's main entrance. Kozshekka suggested we drop off our bags and check-in with the airline before we go to the restaurant. "This way we can hang out at the bar a little longer and you can just walk onto the plane," he said.

"Yeah, man," Felix added. "You could even get rid of the rental car at the same time."

Sounded like a plan to me.

The girls stopped by sometime in the late afternoon to hang out with us until it was time to leave. We packed the car and said our goodbyes to the girls. Somehow, I thought there might be something brewing between Mr. B and Kate, as they lingered a little longer together than most.

Felix and Kozshekka jumped into the Granada and we followed them to the Phoenix airport a little after five o'clock. It was the middle of rush hour, if you could really call it that. We still made it in less than a half hour.

Our first stop was the American Airlines departure terminal, where we checked our bags and got boarding passes for flight 0080 to New York. Our departure time was 11:30 pm with an

ETA of 6:52 am New York time at JFK. It felt great not to worry about our bags or boarding passes. Now unencumbered with luggage or the car, we were ready to boogie and enjoy our last few hours here.

Next stop was the Dollar Rent-A-Car drop-off location, where things went smooth as silk. The car still had a slight hint of beer, even after driving the entire way with the windows open. We left the windows open when returning the car to air out even more. Settling our bill, we bid farewell to the LeBaron, and headed to dinner with Felix and Kozshekka.

The Stockyards Steakhouse was located right off Route 143, across from the airport. We pulled into the parking lot a little after seven, and without a reservation, were relegated to the waiting list. The place was way more high class than we were used to. The waiters were wearing suits and ties, while the Maître d was wearing a tuxedo.

"How many in your party, sir?" the Maître d asked Kozshekka when he approached the podium.

"There's five of us," he responded with a grin. "The name is Stagg, John Stagg. That's two G's, please," he added for emphasis, correcting the Maître d, who had written down "Stag" with one G.

"Thank you, sir," the guy with the name tag of "William" responded, while adding the second "G" to the listing for accuracy. "It's going to be about 40 minutes, Mr. Stagg. You can wait at the bar if you'd like."

"We'd like that very much," Mr. Stagg, I mean Kozshekka, replied.

"Stagg?" I whispered to Mr. B, "Why Stagg?"

"You'll see," he answered with a twinkle in his eye.

We had a couple of drinks at the bar, but I just didn't think I could drink anymore. There were a few shots of Jack Daniels and Peppermint Schnapps (we used to call them 'Snowshoes') with beer chasers to be had while we waited. Bruce took the opportunity to call his brother Peter and remind him of the details for the pickup tomorrow.

During our wait at the bar, the Maître d was calling parties by name over the loudspeaker when their table became available. Finally, about 7:45, we heard him call, "Stagg? Mr. Stagg and party?"

I stood up to leave and Kozshekka pulled me back down to the barstool. "Wait one more second," he said. We sat silently until we heard another announcement.

"Stagg, party of five? Your table is ready. Stagg, party of five?"

It's the simple things in life that I truly enjoy. When we got up to meet the Maître d, Kozshekka winked at him and he realized he'd been had.

We enjoyed a great dinner, probably the best since we started this vacation. The steaks were perfectly cooked, and so were we. I hadn't planned on drinking too much, but it is what it is.

Sometime during dinner, it started to rain outside. Lightly at first, then a total downpour. My fear of flying began to set in, and I certainly wasn't looking forward to taking off in a thunderstorm. Even though we still had more than two hours before our flight, I was getting a little nervous.

I asked Kozshekka about the dangers of flying in the rain, since he was a pilot. He talked about the wind being more of a problem than the rain. "Don't worry, this storm will pass way before you guys take off," he said, "We have a bigger problem than the rain, anyway."

A bigger problem?

# the Flood and the Aftermath

As I looked out the window at the pouring rain, Kozshekka provided us with a previously unknown fact about Phoenix and the Salt River.

"We're in a flash flood zone, man," he said as he pointed out the window. "With this much rain falling this quickly, the roads are going to flood."

"What do you mean, flood?" I asked innocently.

"We ain't going nowhere, sweetheart," said Felix. "Look at the parking lot."

He was right, it was already starting to flood. Many of the remaining diners were also getting up to look. It was raining heavily now, and the water was up to the rims of the tires.

"What are we going to do?" I said to no one in particular.

"Nothing we can do, man," Kozshekka said. "You get used to it out here. It won't last too long, maybe an hour or so. We're here till it clears, so let's order dessert and get another round!"

There was no way to accurately calculate how many beers we may have consumed on this trip, but I put the figure somewhere around 575. I couldn't drink another if I were left stranded in the desert. Well, maybe just one more. This would be my last beer, number 576.

The rain continued to accumulate in the parking lot and then quickly across the road. We could see a few stranded motorists stuck on the road as the water level continued to rise. Kozshekka was right, there was nothing we could do. There was nothing anyone could do.

The restaurant became a party room as the remaining 20 or so diners were in this thing together. People were toasting to the rain and buying each other drinks. The rain continued until about 10 pm, but the water on Route 134 didn't start to recede until almost 11.

"I guess our flight will be delayed," I said to Kozshekka as we paid the bill. The remaining patrons were also getting ready to leave.

"I don't think so," he replied. "It's not raining anymore, and the runways don't flood. There's a good chance your flight goes off on time."

That wasn't good news at all.

We made our way to the parking lot, but now there was traffic on Route 134 going into the airport. We turned into the main entrance at about 11:30, holding out hope that our flight would be delayed. We saw some flights taking off while we were on the access road and heading to the American Airlines departure terminal.

"Oh wow, man," Kozshekka said as he pointed out the window. "I hope that's not your flight, man."

Sure enough, an American Airlines flight was rising from the ground and into the night sky.

The clock at the departure terminal read 11:35 when we found out Kozshekka might have been right. Our flight was no longer at the departure terminal. Although we weren't on it, unfortunately for us, our luggage was.

"Bummer, man," Felix said, as we thanked him and Kozshekka for their hospitality and headed to customer service to see what our options were.

"Oh, I'm so sorry to hear that," Meredith from American Airlines said after we told her what happened. "Let me see what we can do for you." She punched information into the computer terminal as a green glow lit her face in the nearly deserted area of Customer Service.

"I'm sorry," she said with a disappointed look on her face. "We don't have another flight leaving for New York until tomorrow morning at 7:30. Would you like me to book you on that flight?"

I looked at my compadres, who seemed just as beaten as me. We had no car. Even if we called Felix to come back and get us, what were we going to do tomorrow morning? Classes at ASU were starting for them. We were just going to have to curl up in the waiting area for the flight tomorrow morning.

Meredith continued to push buttons on her keyboard while I discussed our situation with Sal and Bruce.

"We really don't have a choice, do we?" I said.

"I better call my brother," Bruce said, reminding us that Peter was our airport pickup. "I hope he can get us later in the day."

"It's almost 3 am in New York," I reminded him. "Your parents are gonna be pissed!"

Just then, Meredith looked up from the terminal and waved me over. "There's a TWA flight heading to New York at 11:52 that I can get you on standby for," she said. "Would you be interested in that? It doesn't get into New York until 10:30 am, though."

"10:30?" I asked. "Why, 10:30? Shouldn't it arrive earlier than that if we're leaving here at midnight?"

"It's not a direct flight," she said. "This TWA flight has a stop in St. Louis."

A TWA flight that stops in St. Louis? What're the chances of that?

"Sure," I said. "Get us on standby for that flight."

We thanked her and rushed over to the TWA waiting area for flight 468 with our trusty standby voucher. They were busy boarding the 11:52 pm flight with ticketed passengers when we got to the desk and checked in. Two other people were waiting with us, also hoping to get on the plane.

Bruce called his house and got his father, who they affectionately called "The Bear," on the phone at 2:45 am New York time. He told him what happened, then held the phone away from his ear so we could all hear.

"How the hell did you assholes miss your goddamn flight! What's going to happen now? What happens if you don't…" Bruce put the phone back to his ear and let The Bear blow off steam.

He explained that we were on standby, but the flight would be TWA instead of American Airlines. If we got on the plane, we would be arriving sometime around 11 am. The Bear noted the change and said he would tell Peter about it. Bruce informed him that when we got off the plane in St. Louis, he would let the phone ring three times to signal all was well. After another round of The Bear yelling into his ear, Bruce hung up the phone.

When all the ticketed passengers were boarded, they called all of us over to the counter, checked us in, and we boarded the plane along with the other two stand-by passengers. Plugging us into the empty seats, we didn't get to sit together and were assigned middle seats ("E") in rows 7, 20, and 21. The next thing I remember was landing in St. Louis, about three hours later.

Although this same plane was going to take us to New York, we had to deplane, and hang out in the waiting area for about 90 minutes. When they were ready to board the plane again, since we were on standby, we were assigned a different set of seats. This time, we got two seats in row 7, and one in row 14. Sal and I took the seats in row 7.

We were so tired at this point, we just wanted to get home. As the captain was welcoming us back on board over the loudspeaker, he explained the skies were clear, and we'd be arriving at New York's LaGuardia Airport around 10:30 am.

LaGuardia Airport?

Did he say LaGuardia Airport?

"Why the fuck are we going to LaGuardia Airport?" I asked a very sleepy Catman.

"Is that what he said?"

"Yes! We're going to LaGuardia Airport, but Peter is going to JFK!"

I hopped out of my seat and went down to row 14, where Mr. B had already settled in and had his eyes closed. "Where is your brother picking us up?" I asked, shaking him awake.

"JFK," he responded, keeping his eyes closed, "Why?"

"Because we're flying to fucking LaGuardia Airport, that's why!"

Now his eyes were open. "Did we get on the wrong plane?"

"Not at all," I said. "This plane was always going to LaGuardia, look at the boarding passes!" I handed him the passes and showed him the destinations, clearly marked as "NYC/LAGUARDIA."

"Well, you were the one holding all the tickets, weren't you?" he pointed out.

He was right, the bastard. I had everything with me because I didn't trust those Hammerheads and was worried about them losing their tickets. I never even noticed.

"I'd say this is your fuckup," he smiled, as he folded his arms and closed his eyes. "You're making that phone call when we get to New York, my friend, not me."

"Don't forget," I said, reminding him of the other minor issue we were facing, "Our luggage was on the plane that went to JFK."

Without opening his eyes, he said, "Well, that's going to be quite another problem, isn't it?"

I woke up somewhere between St. Louis and New York and was surprised how quiet and peaceful the plane was. Most everyone was sleeping or quietly reading. There was no in-flight movie or any other distractions.

I was starting to get the hang of this flying thing. Maybe Mr. B was right—it wasn't that much different than riding a bus.

I sat back down and closed my eyes.

# Epilogue

How did he find us?

    After missing our scheduled flight in Phoenix, lucking out on a stand-by flight with another airline, we landed in a different airport more than three hours later than expected. Somehow, he found us.

We touched down at LaGuardia, but our luggage wasn't on this plane. We had pre-checked it with our original American Airlines flight that landed earlier this morning at JFK without us. There was no reason to go to the baggage claim area, but we would need to make a quick phone call once we got off the plane. Nobody knew we were landing at LaGuardia, including us.

"You're gonna make that phone call to The Bear, Disco," Mr. B demanded as we were standing in the aisle, waiting for the passengers in front of us to gather their things and exit the plane.

"I know, I know," I answered. "Fucking LaGuardia, I can't believe it. How did we miss that? Pete's going to be pissed."

Bruce's brother Peter was one of the strongest people I had ever met. He was a year younger than me but built like a brick shithouse. We would sometimes call him "Ahhhnold" in an accent comparing his physique to bodybuilder Arnold Schwarzenegger. As close brothers, Peter and Bruce were always roughhousing, sometimes even crossing the line into violence. Bruce is as stubborn as can be and would never back down. Peter sometimes doesn't know his own strength, although we all realized he could break any one of us in two.

Peter was aware our TWA flight was arriving at about 10:30, but he didn't know we were at LaGuardia instead of JFK.

Yet there he was, waiting for us.

Leaning against the wall, Peter looked like a gunslinger waiting for the sheriff to show up at High Noon. He used one finger to raise the brim of his baseball hat above eye level and commented smugly, "You fucking Hammerheads landed in LaGuardia?"

Looks like I won't have to make that phone call to The Bear after all.

I was in shock as he reached out to give me a bear hug, doing the same for the Catman. When it was Bruce's turn, instead of giving him a hug, he put him in a headlock, rendering him helpless. Once Mr. B got his footing, he pushed back against Peter and almost knocked him off his feet, earning his release. Bruce might not have the size, but he's tough and wiry, and, as the older brother, he never gives an inch.

Before they could resume their deathmatch, I jumped between them and asked Peter how the hell he found out we were at LaGuardia?

"Disco," he said, "I'm an engineer. I figure shit out."

Peter was studying Chemical Engineering at Clarkson University in upstate New York, near the Canadian border, not far from Montreal. Arriving at JFK and finding no TWA flight 468 from St. Louis listed on the oversized "Arrivals" tote board, he went to customer service and made an inquiry.

"It's not rocket science," he conceded. "Knowing you, Hammerheads, I was just hoping you weren't in Newark."

"Nice work, Kojak," Bruce kidded, then added, "Let's get this show on the road and get our bags." Then he started heading out of the terminal.

"Where the hell are you going?" Pete asked, pointing in the other direction, "Baggage claim is over there."

Uh oh.

"Our bags are at JFK," I said hesitantly, hoping not to set him off on a tirade. "We pre-checked them on our original American Airlines flight, so they landed at JFK without us."

I could see the smoke starting to come out of his ears.

"We've got to go back to JFK?" he asked calmly.

"No shit, Sherlock," Mr. B said, as he turned to run out of the terminal before Peter could reach his throat.

"Oh, he is going to pay for this," Peter guaranteed.

This was going to be a long ride down the Van Wyck Expressway.

On the way, we told Pete about missing our flight and our life and death adventure tubing down the Salt River in Arizona. While approaching the American Airlines arrival terminal, I suggested he wait in the car while we retrieved the luggage.

We walked into the terminal and passed the baggage claim on the left. Part of the area looked like it was under renovation. We located the Customer Service counter further into the building, encountering a middle-aged woman with a name tag identifying her as "Muriel."

"How can I help you boys," she said with a smile.

I explained to her our dilemma, reiterating our tale of woe in Arizona. We had pre-checked our baggage on flight #80, but because of a flood, we missed the plane and it landed here at JFK with our luggage, but without us.

"No problem," she said while leaning into a microphone on the desk. Pressing the button on the neck of the device, she delivered an announcement, "Assistance to the customer service desk, assistance to customer service, please."

Then she smiled at us and said, "It'll just be a moment."

It was a lot longer than just a moment.

She paged for "Assistance" two more times before a beefy guy wearing a red vest showed up to take us down to the baggage claim area. "Frank will take good care of you," she assured us.

Frank's shirt under his vest was stained with what must have been lunch the day before, and his hands and arms were spotted with what looked like white paint. He had a painter's cap on his head that had seen a lot of red, white, and blue splatters in its day. When we arrived in the baggage claim area, everything made sense.

The ceiling in the baggage claim area was being repainted. Dark gray cloth tarps were covering all the chairs, railings, and floors near two of the five baggage claim carousels on the far side. Scattered on the floor were numerous five-gallon containers of white ceiling paint. It must have been getting close to lunch because no one was painting anything when we arrived.

"The lost luggage is in that room," Frank said as he pointed to a red door that was being blocked by a ladder. "If it ain't in there, you'll have to go back to customer service and fill out some forms." Then he walked in the other direction and out of sight.

I made a mental note to tell Muriel that Frank wasn't very helpful at all.

We traversed the baggage claim area, carefully negotiating around the many piles of things covered by the tarps. We arrived at the red door and moved the ladder out of the way. Upon closer inspection, there was a sign affixed to the door painted over with the same red color. You could still read the raised lettering that identified "Lost Luggage."

"What do we do now?" I asked Mr. B, as we stood in front of the door.

"Well, I don't think the door is going to open itself," he said, "You want me to say, 'Open Sesame'?"

"That's not what I meant, dickhead," I replied, "I thought there would be someone manning a desk or making sure nobody just walks in and takes what they want. Don't we have to give them our luggage check ticket or something?"

"Maybe they're inside?" the Catman proposed.

I guess that was possible, so I reached for the doorknob, half expecting it to be locked. Instead, it opened into a darkened room that contained musty air. The confined atmosphere wasted no time escaping through the now opened portal. I blindly reached for a light switch near the door frame, finding a double switch. Soon, the room was bathed in slightly flickering fluorescent light.

At first glance, it seemed like we were the first people in this room for months. The rectangular room contained a row of metallic shelves to the right, holding about a dozen or so suitcases of varying shapes, sizes, and colors. They were covered in a layer of dust and cobwebs that would be more suited for an Indiana Jones movie.

Scattered on the floor were more suitcases. Some were

standing neatly together in groups, others in varying stages of disarray. It was as if the last person searching for luggage was rummaging through the room like a criminal looking for hidden jewels.

"Jesus H. Christ." The Catman commented.

"You have got to be fucking kidding me," I remarked.

"This shit has been in here for months," Mr. B observed as he walked around the room, purposely kicking over some of the standing luggage. "Our bags ain't in here, I can tell you that."

No argument from me.

"I gotta get out of here, man," I said. "I'm getting the heebie-jeebies. Let's go back and give Muriel the business. There is no way our luggage is in here."

"My camera and film are in my suitcase," the Catman remembered. "You know how many pictures of chick's asses I have in there?"

Talk about your Greek Tragedy.

I shut off the lights and sealed the "Tomb of the Lost Luggage" again for the next dumb schmuck, then started to navigate around the mounds covered with tarps as we made our way back to Customer Service. On this trip, we faced adversity at almost every turn, but we triumphed, in the end, every time.

I just wasn't sure how we were going to get out of this one.

Like the Catman, I also packed a camera and a couple rolls of film in my suitcase. Only it was my father's camera, not mine. It was also the only decent piece of luggage my parents owned. I was going to get my ass kicked for sure.

While walking past one pile, I noticed a red-colored suitcase peeking out from the bottom of the tarp.

Why would there be a suitcase in the middle of the floor covered by a tarp?

Like a magician uncovering his final illusion for the crowd, I removed the tarp off the pile and exposed our three bags!

"Oh, boys…" I yelled to get the attention of Mr. B and the Catman, "Look what I found!"

"Are you fucking kidding me!" Mr. B yelled back.

Just then, Peter burst into the baggage claim area shouting, "Let's go, man. They already told me twice to move the car, or they were going to tow me and the car."

"Keep your shirt on, we're coming," Mr. B said, as he calmly walked towards him, reaching out with his left hip, like a hockey player, and knocking him off his feet. Peter chased him out of the terminal, screaming obscenities.

Once safely in the car, I strategically sat in the front seat so there would be no more public displays of violence between the two brothers. We regaled Peter with the ups and downs of our time in LA and San Diego, including how Bruce found weed in the LAX bathroom and how it had been stolen from us.

As if on cue, Springsteen's "Promised Land" came on WNEW-FM, and we told him about our "Springsteen Burn" pact.

"Too bad we're out of hooch," Bruce said from the back seat.

"Who said we're out of hooch?" Peter replied while grinning, reaching into his shirt pocket, and producing a nicely rolled doobie. "Anyone got a light?"

With the Catman providing a torch, we all sang along to the chorus of, "Mister, I ain't a boy, no, I'm a man!"

Yeah, this trip turned out to be one of the best times I ever had. It was undoubtedly the most memorable. Good times and good friends, but I was happy to be home. There's something about familiar surroundings that makes you feel warm and fuzzy. No more worries about getting lost on unfamiliar freeways or drowning in rivers.

We were finally home.

As we exited the airport onto the Belt Parkway towards Long Island, the Catman was pointing to the shoulder area of the road and shouting, "What the fuck is that?"

Sure enough, a tall, thin man with long brown hair streaked with grey was casually strolling on the grassy shoulder of the road, walking toward the traffic. He had a long, mostly grey beard, and a massive smile on his face, seemingly without a care in the world.

He was balls-out, naked, with a half-chub waving in the wind.

Peter beeped the horn, and he responded with a friendly wave back.

"I guess we're officially back in New York," Mr. B deadpanned.

Oh, how right he was.

It was good to be home…

# Afterword

So that's the story, dear reader.

It's a story Bruce, Sal, and I have been telling friends and family since the day we got back from that trip in 1978. I don't think a single year has gone by when I didn't tell someone, some part of this story. It's especially delightful when telling bits and pieces to people who have never heard the tale before. Whenever small talk turns to *The Tonight Show* or Johnny Carson, I jump in with that part of the story. If someone mentions a flight delay or arriving at their destination without a reservation, I tell that part of the story. When people start talking about tubing in a river, well, you get the idea.

We've always had a PG-13 version of the story for the kids when they were young. However, regaling them and their friends with the R-rated version of the story was much more enjoyable as they became adults. Quite frankly, most people can't believe all these things actually happened.

But they did.

After over 40 years of telling the story in bits and pieces, I decided to sit down and compile the narrative in its entirety. It's my first book, so be gentle with me.

I thought you might want to catch up with some of these Hammerheads and what they are doing today.

My cousin, Sal "The Catman," has lived in New Jersey for a long time. He still reminds me that no matter how hard I try, I can never catch up to him in age. He'll always be three months older than me. That's why when we were kids living next door to each other in the East New York section of Brooklyn, I was always Robin to his Batman. And I'm OK with that. He has never been a cousin, always a brother to me. I'm not sure if he will ever retire, but if you live near Aberdeen, New Jersey, he might still be delivering your mail.

I've known Bruce ("Mr. B") since I walked into A Capella Choir in 10th Grade. I was a little bit of a nerdy kid, and he was a senior. We were complete opposites. Although our group of friends would grow over the next few years, Bruce and I seemed to always be in the middle of all these adventures. I don't think there has been a story I've told throughout my adult life that didn't include Mr. B in some way, shape, or form.

Our professional careers began together, working at Goldwater Hospital on Roosevelt Island, which sits in the middle of the East River. We have been part of Healthcare IT ever since. A semi-retired IT Consultant living in Mount Sinai here on Long Island, he's about to get his Medicare Card and his first Social Security check. Hey Bruce, you made it!

I made it back out to California in 2016 while attending an IT Conference in San Diego. I met up with my cousin John who, at the time, was responsible for the distribution of Anheuser Busch products to all of Southern California. Now he's a Director for the Ballast Point Brewing Company and living in Spring Valley, California, a suburb of San Diego.

My other cousin Tony is the founder and Executive Director of the Lombardi Family Office, which supports small businesses and the families that own them. They provide services and solutions to help the families and their businesses to reach their ultimate potential. He also does public speaking at schools, churches and conferences.

Currently living on the beach in Carlsbad, California (between Los Angeles and San Diego), Tony's a published author and integrates spiritual teaching from the bible into his speaking engagements.

As far as I know, he no longer owns any snakes …

My Uncle Mickey died in 1986, and I haven't seen my Aunt Lillian since our trip.

Felix and Kozshekka, our two crazy friends from Arizona, went on to successful careers in aviation. Kozshekka is pondering retiring from the FAA after over 38 years. Felix retired after 32 years with American Airlines, piloting jumbo jets. I'm sure some of you out there have been lucky enough to be his passenger at one time or another.

For those of you that have the complete DVD Box set of *The Tonight Show Starring Johnny Carson*, check out the show from August 17, 1978. Yep, that's us interrupting the monologue and getting burned by The King on National television.

As far as Jo Anne from Travel Mood? Let's just say I never did send her that Christmas Card.

I've been fortunate to have been associated with the same group of friends since college. Over the years, we've participated in many adventures. This story was centered on a West Coast trip with just my cousin Sal (the Catman) and my friend Bruce (Mr. B). However, most of the people you were introduced to in the first chapter (The Going Away Party) have been part of their own adventures.

We formed a tight-knit group for a couple of years (1977-1982) spending every waking hour doing some crazy things. We are all still good friends to this day.

We spent a whole summer traveling around the Tri-State area, seeing Bruce Springsteen live shows at different venues. Some of us even got to meet him not long after we returned from this trip. We've traveled to different places to see hockey games or visit other friends to ski (even though we never skied). Every trip was an adventure, and every trip included a different set of participants.

If you thought this trip was crazy, every one of those other adventures resulted in even more outlandish situations and circumstances.

Who knows, maybe if enough of you enjoy this book, I'll take the time to tell some of those other stories.

Wouldn't that be fun?

# Acknowledgments

A lot of work goes into trying to chronicle a story that is over 40 years old, but writing it was the easiest part. To be honest, I don't know how anyone ever wrote a book before having access to the Internet.

Trying to jog the memories of my comrades in this book about events from 40-plus years ago was daunting, at best. Not only did we not remember a lot of the details, what we did remember was sometimes conflicting information. Quite frankly, I don't know how Bruce and Sal put up with me over the course of writing this book.

Thank goodness for my actual source materials. For some reason, I still had receipts, itineraries, plane tickets and notes from this trip in a "box of memories." Amazingly, I don't have anything from any other trip or adventure with my friends, other than pictures that automatically prevent us from ever becoming a Supreme Court Justice. Yet, I saved mementos from this trip as if I knew, someday, they would come in handy when writing a book.

I hope you enjoyed all the chapter illustrations drawn by the master, John Colquhoun. I've known John since we worked together at The Campus Slate, the weekly student newspaper at the New York Institute of Technology from 1978-1980 He built himself a very successful career as an art director and illustrator for over 30 years. His illustrations have been associated with national retailers like Little Caeser's Pizza (he drew the guy), Wendy's and The Outback Steakhouse.

When I first began writing the book, I thought it would be fun to use pictures or illustrations at the beginning of each chapter. John's ability to capture a single moment from each chapter is on display, allowing you to smile before you have even read a single word.

Check out his illustrations and animations on his website at: http://jcolquhoun.com/index.asp

Although John now categorizes himself as semi-retired while living in Hillsdale, NY, he's currently working with Andy Landorf on an internet comic strip called, "The New 60." You can find it at: https://www.thenew60comic.com/

If it weren't for Valentina Janek and the Long Island Breakfast Club (LIBC), I may have never taken this journey. I attended an LIBC meeting with intentions of writing a column on the fantastic work they were doing in helping "older" Long Islanders who found themselves out of work. At one of their monthly "networking" events, I met many people who had turned to writing and were having books published after leaving (or being forced out of) their careers in the business world.

That's where I met Stephanie Larkin from Red Penguin Books and attended a Long Island Writer's Club (LIWC) meeting. Her enthusiasm and confidence, along with conversations I had with other published writers, was the impetus for writing this book.

After making the decision to join Red Penguin and write the book, we were hit with COVID-19. Suddenly, I had a lot more time on my hands with very few distractions.

Of course, that meant my wife Barbara had to put up with me being sequestered in my room at all hours of the day and night. Without her love and support, this would have never been completed. She is the best editor I've ever worked with. She cuts to the point and never blows smoke up my ass. If she doesn't like something, I don't believe anyone would like it.

I've always looked forward after making key decisions in my life, never looking back. Except this one. I always look back at the decision to marry her in 1983 as the best one I ever made.  Love ya, honey!

www.PaulDiSclafani.com

# About the Author

Paul DiSclafani is an award-winning columnist for the Anton News Group, which publishes local newspapers in Nassau County on Long Island, in New York. As a weekly columnist for the Massapequa Observer since 2016, his column "Long Island Living" has garnered several writing awards.

The Press Club of Long Island recognized "Long Island Living" in the "Best Column" category in both 2018 (Third Place) and 2020 (Second Place). The New York Press Association voted "Long Island Living" as one of the best humor columns in all of New York State (Third Place) in 2020.

A Massapequa resident since 1967, Paul had his roots in the East New York section of Brooklyn, growing up surrounded by a large Italian family. Many of his columns and musings recall family gatherings and touch on all aspects of life today.

Paul began his love affair with the printed word after taking a journalism class during his senior year in High School. That led to a successful writing career in college as a sportswriter and editor. Although pursuing a career in the world of Healthcare IT, he continued to make friends and colleagues chuckle with stories and tales (both written and verbal) through the years.

Ironically, it was a sports blog that got him back into writing in 2015. His daily articles on the Mets run to a World Series in 2015 got the juices flowing again. After continuing to write into 2016, he submitted a sports-related story to the Massapequa Observer, beginning a new career. He began submitting several essays and musings about life on Long Island. After just a few weeks, the editors were requesting something every week.

Having told stories over the years of adventures with his friends, and even chronicling them in short story form, he decided to finally sit down and write a book about one of them. "Burning Through the West Coast" is the culmination of those years of storytelling.

A married father of two, Paul and his wife Barbara have been blessed with two great kids, James and Kevin.

You can read his Long Island Living columns on the Massapequa Observer website at:

https://www.massapequaobserver.com/author/paul-disclafani/

Awards:

- 2018 Press Club of Long Island: Best Column (Third Place) "Long Island Living"
- 2020 Press Club of Long Island: Best Column (Second Place) "Long Island Living"
- 2020 Press Club of Long Island: Best Humor Column (Third Place) "My Stupid House"
- 2020 New York Press Association: Best Humor Column (Third Place) "Long Island Living"

www.ingramcontent.com/pod-product-compliance
Lightning Source LLC
LaVergne TN
LVHW051051080426
835508LV00019B/1818